Liberalism at Wits' End

Liberalism at Wits' End

*The Libertarian Revolt
against the Modern State*

STEPHEN L. NEWMAN

———————

Cornell University Press
Ithaca and London

First published 1984 by Cornell University Press.
Published in the United Kingdom by Cornell University Press Ltd., London.

International Standard Book Number 0-8014-1747-3
Library of Congress Catalog Card Number 84-7108

Printed in the United States of America

*Librarians: Library of Congress cataloging information
appears on the last page of the book.*

*The paper in this book is acid-free and meets the guidelines
for permanence and durability of the Committee on Production
Guidelines for Book Longevity of the Council on Library Resources.*

To my mother,
in memory of my father

Contents

Preface

To a group of radical individualists in the United States, big government is incompatible with liberty. Their complaint is less original than timely. The libertarian revolt against the modern state is launched on a rising tide of antistatist sentiment among the American public.

Our large national state with its sprawling bureaucracy and interventionist policies is a relatively recent development. Not so long ago most citizens lived out their lives virtually undisturbed by the government in Washington. Today's nostalgia for that time is born of a general dissatisfaction with the performance of the modern state. Arguments long thought settled by the New Deal legacy are suddenly reopened and shown to have electoral potency. Not surprisingly, political strategists have rediscovered the virtues of the minimal state. So have professional philosophers, and new articles on old questions fill the scholarly journals. After forty years, libertarian ideas are once again part of the American mainstream. Yet libertarians themselves stand outside the mainstream. Their object is not reform but revolution; they demand the abolition of all government intervention in the lives and affairs of a free people.

Libertarian thought is distinctive among contemporary ide-
ologies. Embracing both right-wing and left-wing objections to
the use and abuse of state power, it offers a critical perspective on
the putatively benign paternalism practiced by liberals and the
aggressive militarism advocated by conservatives. At its best,
libertarianism invites a much-needed reassessment of state power
and purposes from the perspective of human liberty. The libertarian critique of the state rests ultimately, however, on the (classical) liberal reading of liberty as the inviolable right of property.
Consequently, libertarian sensitivity to the abuse of power
abruptly disappears at the entrance to the marketplace.

The libertarian revolt is a sign of the times, suggesting what
others have called a crisis of public authority. Modern government, undermined by its own dubious achievements and admit-
ted failures, suffers a loss of legitimacy. Libertarian antistatism
addresses the current crisis in the language of America's liberal
tradition. It amplifies and resonates familiar Lockean themes in
an attempt to give them new brilliance, forcing us to confront
the seeming contradiction between our liberal principles and our
statist practices. A Lockean defense of individual rights still has
power to persuade, but the libertarians' refusal to carry that defense beyond a narrowly construed political realm into the economic arena makes clear the inadequacy of their argument. Perhaps in the seventeenth century Locke had no need to address the
effects of concentrated economic power. Today, however, no
discussion of human freedom can afford to ignore them.

The true significance of libertarianism lies not in its contributions to political theory or practical politics but in what it represents as an expression of the liberal imagination. In libertarianism, the American liberal tradition comes full circle. The activist
state erected to serve Lockean ends is condemned for having
violated its own first principles. Unmindful of the increase in
private power which rivals the growth of public authority, libertarianism proposes to return America to its original condition
(from the standpoint of freedom) by curtailing the size and scope
of government. It is at best a partial solution; at worst it amounts
to a betrayal of liberty and the sacrifice of human rights to the

right of property. Libertarianism takes Locke out of context and confuses the present with the past. It calls for the renewal of liberal theory, but it demonstrates liberalism at wits' end.

Surprisingly little has been written about the libertarian movement. Although the political philosophy of Robert Nozick, perhaps the best-known libertarian, has been subjected to numerous studies, to my knowledge this book is the first to examine the broad range of libertarian theories. My interest in libertarianism developed quite by accident. As a graduate student immersed in late-eighteenth-century British radicalism, I had the good fortune to be offered a fellowship in residence at the Institute for Humane Studies at Menlo Park, California. I learned only after I arrived there that the institute was a libertarian organization. My conversations with the staff made me curious about their beliefs, in which I came to see similarities to the older radicalism I was studying. Eventually I abandoned the pursuit of radicals in eighteenth-century Britain and turned to libertarians in the twentieth-century United States. This book has grown out of that early enterprise.

I am grateful to the institute for supporting my research, and I am especially indebted to Leonard Liggio and Kenneth Templeton, then its director, for introducing me to libertarianism. Though we disagree on many points, I have great respect for both men and found them to be delightful colleagues during the year I spent in Menlo Park. Major funding for my work was provided by the Cornell University Center for the Study of the American Political Economy. Additional funding was supplied by Ripon College.

I owe a rather large intellectual debt, for this book has profited from the advice and comments of many friends. I wish first to thank my teachers at Cornell, Isaac Kramnick, Theodore Lowi, and Eldon Eisenach. From them I first learned to appreciate the ambiguities of the liberal tradition and the many ironies of American politics. If my efforts here contribute in some small way to our understanding of American liberalism, it is because I have built on their insights. Benjamin Ginsberg has my thanks along with the others for seeing the book in its early incarnation and supporting it in its revised form. There would have been no book to publish were it not for the suggestion of Leonard Hochberg, who encouraged me to investigate libertarianism and generously devoted hours to discussions of my research. Through several rewrites I have also benefited from comments by William T. Bluhm, Nathan Schwartz, and Booth Fowler. Don Herzog's page-by-page critique of the penultimate draft has spared me much embarrassment. The final version was also improved by the suggestions of an anonymous reader. I alone, of course, must bear full responsibility for any defects that remain.

Lawrence Malley of Cornell University Press has my sincere gratitude for his enthusiastic support of this project. I am also grateful to Barbara Salazar for her assistance in readying the manuscript for publication. Finally, I thank my colleagues on the second floor of East Hall for their patience and good humor, and for providing such a congenial environment in which to work.

STEPHEN L. NEWMAN

Ripon, Wisconsin

Liberalism at Wits' End

I

The Significance of
Libertarianism

After 1937, the Constitution did not die from the Roosevelt
revolution, as many had predicted, but the basis for the liberal-
conservative dialogue did die. Liberalism-conservatism as the
source of public philosophy no longer made any sense. Once the
principle of positive government in an indeterminable but expanding political sphere was established, criteria arising out of
the very issue of expansion became irrelevant.
—THEODORE J. LOWI, *The End of Liberalism*

THERE was a time, not long ago, when Americans looked
hopefully to their government in Washington for solutions. Today many people see that government as the chief source of our
nation's problems. Big government, with its sprawling bureaucratic apparatus and miles of red tape, has become a symbol of
waste, inefficiency, and arbitrariness. Its fine-tuning of the economy has not been able to find a balance between inflation and
high unemployment. Its social programs and welfare policies
have engendered resentment among the middle class. Politically
the time is ripe for a revolt against the modern state, and the
libertarian movement, armed with newly fashionable political
theories, is ready to lead the assault.

How serious is the libertarian revolt? In the 1980 presidential
election the Libertarian party's candidate, Ed Clark, received
over one million votes. That makes his party the third largest in
the United States. Libertarians confidently predict they will have
an electoral majority before the year 2000.

What do libertarians want? Their party platform calls for an end to government intervention in the economy, the repeal of all laws touching on morality and other private conduct, and rejection of an interventionist foreign policy. More broadly, the libertarian movement seeks the dissolution of the modern state.

Libertarianism attracts adherents from the left and the right, from the establishment and the counterculture. It unites opposites—business people and hippies, pacifists and survivalists, male chauvinists and feminists—who can agree on their right to be left alone. Its intellectual appeal lies in its theoretical coherence and logical consistency. Equipped with a rigorous critique of state power, libertarians do not merely protest government policies; they question the fundamental legitimacy of government itself.

Libertarianism represents a significant challenge to "politics as usual" in the United States. That challenge is not primarily electoral, for the Libertarian party is as yet a minor threat to the two-party system. Rather, libertarianism poses an ideological challenge. It comes at a time when most Americans are ideologically disarmed, angry at the status quo but lacking an alternative vision. The libertarian movement offers the dissatisfied a framework for utopia that many people find compelling. Though the libertarian alternative is gravely flawed, it deserves to be treated seriously, for its defects have implications that touch on the philosophic foundations of the American polity.

To appreciate the significance of libertarianism, we must view it against the background of America's Lockean political culture. The United States is the premier Lockean polity. Its founding was virtually an acting out of the principles of Locke's *Second Treatise of Government,* and for almost one hundred years the nation seemed a near-perfect model of what Locke meant by civil society. Government in America was instituted to protect life and property. Authority was purposefully limited and made subject to multiple restraints in order to safeguard the liberty of the people. Fortunate material circumstances, notably an abundant supply of free land, allowed equal opportunity and virtual autonomy for (almost) all (not, of course, for blacks, Indians, or women). Free-market capitalism, nurtured by the state, served the interests of rich and poor alike by opening the avenue of success to ambition and talent. This is the political heritage cherished by modern libertarians.

The course of events, however, worked the transformation of American politics. The policy of laissez-faire passed into history with the rise of the corporation, the concentration of capital, and the emergence of monopoly and oligopoly at the turn of the century. Around the same time, the closing of the frontier and the introduction of wage labor on a large scale deprived most Americans of the independence enjoyed by their nineteenth-century counterparts. It became clear that political and economic liberty could no longer guarantee personal autonomy or equal opportunity. The unique conditions that had made America a Lockean polity almost without effort finally disappeared. To this point Americans had taken their Lockean values for granted; now they were forced to confront their situation.

The changed conditions brought a new politics and the expansion of state power. Both the privileged and the dispossessed sought and received some measure of government assistance in the form of economic regulation. Yet, however loud the cry for reform, the nation never abandoned its Lockean faith. Socialism won few adherents among the working class, and big business, despite its new appreciation of government regulation, held fast to the distinction between state and society. In its own self-image, the United States would remain a liberal polity. Even as the state grew in size and power, it was pledged to Lockean ends. This is the paradox of liberal statism.

The twentieth century brought the Great Depression and the New Deal, America's first truly significant deviation from Locke in the practice of government. Afterward the role of government continued to expand in response to social and economic pressures. The modern state assumed new and lasting responsibility for the welfare of society; however, it had neither the institutional capacity nor the ideological basis for centralized planning. Instead, as recent scholarship has documented, policy making effectively fell into the hands of those private interests that were best able to make their demands heard and their influence felt.

This state of affairs was believed to further democracy insofar as the sum of those interests was believed to embody the public good.[1] As numerous critics have pointed out, the flaw in this approach to practical government is that not all interests are equally influential. The much-discussed democratic explosion of the 1960s that resulted in the dramatic expansion of the welfare state (and thereby helped to create the present notorious image of big government) came about only when for reasons of political expedience the channels of access were opened to groups previously excluded by virtue of their relative powerlessness.[2]

Lacking a will of its own, the modern liberal state seems less a mighty (and threatening) leviathan than a political weathercock; it takes direction from the prevailing breezes and is ill prepared to resist the winds of change. Consequently, the size and shape of contemporary American government to a large degree reflect the range of demands placed upon it. The phenomenon of liberal statism provides a formula for the growth of government effectively without limit and to no particular end.[3] Unfortunately, public resources are not unlimited, nor can all societal interests be accommodated at once without contradiction. Because the liberal state lacks criteria for allocating scarce resources among competing claimants and for competing purposes, it is doomed to suffer incoherence and failure in its attempts to satisfy all parties. So it is that American government has arrived at an impasse, and public discontent with the current state of affairs threatens public authority with a loss of legitimacy.

Striking in this context is the absence of any serious alternative to the status quo originating with the major political parties. Their adherence to politics as usual testifies to the ideological poverty of mainstream American politics. The fact is that neither the Republicans nor the Democrats find it in their interest to challenge the statist consensus. Each benefits by serving as a bridge between private interests and public power. In this respect American politics has changed a great deal over the past fifty years. Before the New Deal, "liberals" and "conservatives" (both arguing within the value framework of Locke's philosophy) earnestly debated the propriety of government intervention. Within the terms of that debate it was possible to assess critically the consequences of expanding the role of the state with a seriousness that our casual acceptance of statism negates. The political triumph of liberal statism in the twentieth century obliterated the principled distinction between liberals and conservatives. Today, as a leading student of American politics remarks, "the most important difference between liberals and conservatives, Republicans and Democrats, is to be found in the interest groups they identify with."[4]

Antistatism has not been without modern-day champions, but for the most part they have occupied the lunatic fringe of public discourse. Now the libertarian movement, responding to popular dissatisfaction with the performance of government, is attempting to win a new respectability for the antistatist position. Libertarianism offers the principled opposition to liberal statism long absent from American public life.

At first glance the libertarian movement can be mistaken for an attempted revival of the Old Right crusade against the New Deal. It preaches much the same brand of economics and even borrows the rhetoric of that earlier revolt against the state. Like the anti–New Dealers, libertarians associate statism with collectivism (the subordination of the individual to the group) and socialism. Libertarians, however, are not merely economic conservatives nostalgic for the free market. Their movement is also more broadly anti-authoritarian. It condemns American imperialism in language reminiscent of the student left of the 1960s. And it is as quick to defend alternative lifestyles as it is to criticize government regulation of the workplace. Gays, feminists, black separatists, environmentalists, survivalists, and other such groups are all welcome in the libertarian camp. Libertarianism offers to countercultural radicals and other dissenters from the American mainstream the option of cultural laissez-faire. The libertarian movement also protests governmental invasion of privacy and campaigns against so-called victimless crimes, such as drug use, gambling, and prostitution, which penalize consensual or entirely self-regarding acts.

The dominant theme of the libertarian movement is individual liberty. Libertarians identify themselves as heirs to the tradition of classical liberalism, which they believe has fallen into neglect. They blame the intelligentsia for ignoring liberal principles and flirting with the statist heresy. Now if statism is to be defeated, liberty must again be made a central concern of politicians and thinkers alike. In the words of Friedrich Hayek, the building of a free society must once more be made a living intellectual issue capable of challenging society's liveliest minds. What is needed to counter statist influence is a liberal utopia, "a truly liberal radicalism . . . which is not too severely practical and which does not confine itself to what appears today as politically possible."[5] Hayek's truly liberal radicalism is what libertarianism is supposed to be.

In essence, then, the libertarian revolt against the modern state is a reflexive Lockean response to the failure of liberal statism. It seeks in effect to begin the American experiment over again. The question before us is whether this is truly a new beginning or a dead end. The answer will have profound implications for the future of the liberal tradition in America.

2

The Ideological Origins
of the Libertarian Revolt

If you wish to know how libertarians regard the State and any of
its acts, simply think of the State as a criminal band, and all of
the libertarian attitudes will logically fall into place.

—MURRAY ROTHBARD, *For a New Liberty*

THE twin pillars of libertarian ideology are antistatism and capitalism. The two are closely connected, since libertarians view
the modern state as the enemy of the free market. Far from
providing necessary protection to market actors—the tradi-
tionally legitimate role of the minimal or "night-watchman"
state of classical liberalism—government, libertarians charge,
now aspires to omnipotence. It dictates to individuals in matters
of personal conduct and morality, tells them how to run their
business, and then divides the profits among the undeserving in
the name of social justice. With like disregard of individual liberty, the state compels men to bear arms in its service and wages
aggressive war on others of its kind. Accordingly, libertarians (in
the words of their party platform) "challenge the cult of the
omnipotent state and defend the rights of the individual." Trans-
lated into specific demands, this "challenge" is a call to dismantle
government in America. The Libertarian party wants to abolish
the entire federal regulatory apparatus along with social security,
welfare, public education, and the powers of taxation and eminent domain. Insisting on the right of all persons "to live in
whatever manner they choose," so long as their actions do not
forcibly interfere with the like right of others, the party asks the
repeal of all drug, sex, and consumer-protection laws. Believing

with Randolph Bourne that war is the health of the state, libertarians would have the United States withdraw from the United Nations, terminate its foreign commitments, and reduce its military establishment to a minimal defensive force.

The various themes sounded by the libertarian platform are familiar to the student of American politics. What is unusual is to find these themes sung in harmony. Opposition to big government (when conceived of as the welfare state) and the pairing of capitalism and freedom are postures typical of the American right, which holds fast to the classical liberal conception of the state. On the other hand, opposition to the military establishment and the association of personal liberty with "experiments in living" seem characteristic of the American left, which selectively prefers the legacy of John Stuart Mill to other facets of the liberal tradition. At a glance, libertarianism appears, paradoxically, to be both conservative and radical at the same time. More accurately, it appears simultaneously to embrace elements of the liberal tradition not usually joined together in the American context.

Libertarians delight in their failure to conform to an ideological stereotype. They advertise themselves as having transcended the conventional left-right continuum of American politics, not by an eclectic borrowing of positions but through commitment to a set of logically coherent political principles. Libertarian theorist Murray Rothbard boils the libertarian creed down to one central axiom, which states that no person or group of persons may aggress against the life or property of another.[1] Under this rule neither the state nor any private party may initiate or threaten the use of force against any person for any purpose. Only by voluntary agreement (that is, contractual obligation) do free men and women regulate their conduct and dispose of their possessions.

There has always been an antistatist tradition in American politics; libertarianism is simply one of its most recent manifestations. The American Revolution was fueled in large measure by the colonists' fear of a British (that is, governmental) plot to subvert their traditional liberties. The Whig ideology that informed their views presented a cyclical notion of history inherited from classical antiquity. In this scheme of things even the best government was and would always be prone to corruption and likely to degenerate into tyranny.[2] So naturally the Founding Fathers were a skeptical lot who, when it came time to design a government of their own, hemmed it in with constitutional restrictions and set the various departments as checks on one another's power. The Revolutionary pamphleteer Tom Paine may well have captured the spirit of his age when he wrote that "society in every state is a blessing, but government even in its best state is but a necessary evil."[3]

The Founding Fathers were for the most part optimistic Whigs who hoped that America might prove to be a historical exception and remain forever uncorrupted. But it was not long before some people were again alarmed by the specter of tyrannical government. The Jeffersonians saw the framework of an oppressive state in Federalist policies. Later, John C. Calhoun and his allies raised the banner of states' rights against the perceived threat of a centralized national government under northern domination. Abolitionists were equally ready to damn the government as a villain for its support of slavery in the South. More than half a century after the Revolution the words of Tom Paine were echoed by Henry David Thoreau, who said of government that it is "at best an expedient," adding that "most governments are usually, and all governments are sometimes, inexpedient."[4]

Although a healthy suspicion of government has been central to our political life as a nation, the radical antistatist tradition has been a dissenting and ultimately marginal viewpoint. One need only think of Thoreau, who advised good men to break bad laws, to let their lives become "a counter friction to stop the machine."[5] For all his radicalism, Thoreau was hardly a political animal—his words were directed at the individual, not the mass—and his philosophy never became a force in mainstream politics. Thoreau's was an appeal to conscience, not a call for mobilization.

Radical antistatism was given even more vigorous expression by Thoreau's lesser-known contemporary Lysander Spooner.

Spooner, a Boston lawyer and abolitionist, is revered by today's libertarians. He ran a successful private postal service until the government forced him out of business. Ever an unyielding critic of the state, he authored a series of pamphlets attacking the Constitution as an invalid (and hence void) social contract. In his eyes government had much in common with a highwayman, except that of the two the highwayman was the more honorable.

> The highwayman takes solely upon himself the responsibility, danger, and crime of his own act. He does not pretend that he has any rightful claim to your money, or that he intends to use it for your own benefit. He does not pretend to be anything but a robber. . . . Furthermore, having taken your money, he leaves you, as you wish him to do. He does not persist in following you on the road, against your will; assuming to be your rightful "sovereign," on account of the "protection" he affords you. He does not keep "protecting" you, by commanding you to bow down and serve him; by requiring you to do this, and forbidding you to do that; by robbing you of more money as often as he finds it for his interest or pleasure to do so; and by branding you as a rebel, a traitor, and an enemy to your country, and shooting you down without mercy, if you dispute his authority, or resist his demands. He is too much of a gentleman to be guilty of such impostures, and insults, and villainies as these. In short, he does not, in addition to robbing you, attempt to make you either his dupe or his slave.[6]

Spooner's ideas were seconded by Stephen Pearl Andrews, Benjamin R. Tucker, and others in an obscure network of radical individualists that flourished briefly in the nineteenth century.[7] To modern libertarians, these men are true culture heroes.

If the libertarians are, as they claim, heirs to the antistatist tradition represented by the likes of Paine, Thoreau, and Spooner, they are even more clearly heirs to the legacy of Albert Jay Nock, one of the New Deal's most bitter opponents. As an unreconstructed "conservative" of the laissez-faire school, Nock greeted the New Deal with a gloomy assessment of America's future. "What we and our more nearly immediate descendants shall see," he predicted in 1935, "is a steady progress in collectivism running into a military despotism of a severe type."[8] Nock foresaw ever-increasing centralization, a steadily growing bureaucracy, and increased political control of the marketplace culminating in a state-managed economy so corrupt and inefficient as to require a system of forced labor. Believing it was impossible to turn the tide of statism, he addressed his dire prophecy to "the remnant," those remaining individualists of future generations, however few, whose task it would be to perpetuate the true principles of liberty.

It would not be inaccurate to characterize the libertarian movement as Nock's remnant. The libertarian world view has been shaped in response to the New Deal and the rise of the welfare state—the dramatic growth of social programs and entitlements in the 1960s that vastly expanded the size and scope of government. Ideologically, libertarianism owes a profound debt to Nock and other early critics of the new positive state, including Nock's disciple Frank Chodorov, Henry Hazlitt, Milton Friedman, and Friedrich Hayek.[9] In this respect libertarianism is linked to that branch of American "conservatism" that clings to the doctrines of classical political economy and regards the acceptance of Keynesianism as the first step on the road to serfdom.

The emergence of libertarianism as a distinct ideology is a relatively recent phenomenon. Small circles of self-described libertarians first began to appear in the late 1950s. Most often they could be found on college campuses under the tutelage of such conservative economists as Friedrich Hayek, Milton Friedman, and Murray Rothbard. Libertarian ideas were initially conveyed to a broader audience through the novels of Ayn Rand, whose Objectivist movement enjoyed considerable popularity throughout the 1960s. Rand, a refugee from the Soviet Union, was a self-styled philosopher whose moral and political arguments are woven into the fabric of her very successful novels. Rand's fiction characteristically portrays a superior individual, naturally and properly an egoist, locked in battle with the forces of collectivism (usually the state), which would impose upon him the self-denying and ultimately self-destructive doctrine of altruism. More is at stake in the outcome of this battle than his personal fate, for the Randian hero is really Nietzsche's superman in the guise of capitalist entrepreneur. He is the creator of all value, the source of all wealth, the instrument of human progress. His destruction means the end of Western civilization.* Rand developed a cult following, especially among the young. In the years following the publication of *Atlas Shrugged* (1957), Objectivist societies devoted to the study of her "philosophy" appeared on campuses across the nation. In the same period, Rand took to elaborating her views in the pages of the *Objectivist Newsletter,* a tabloid featuring essays on themes first presented in her novels, and offered seminars on Objectivism at the Nathaniel Branden Institute, a think tank of sorts set up by her most devoted disciple. Convinced that she had obtained a direct knowledge of objective reality, Rand was never tolerant of those who questioned her views. She perceived a world of black and white, good and evil, where individuals must choose between truth and self-delusion. Speaking through the mouth of one of her characters in *Atlas Shrugged,* she explained, "There are two sides to every issue: one side is right and the other is wrong, but the middle is always evil."[10] Rand's Objectivism admits no compromise. Over time Rand became increasingly dogmatic, insisting that her followers accept her opinions on matters large and small. Cigarette smoking, for example, was thought by Rand to be life-enhancing, and she had little regard for nonsmokers. In like manner, she dismissed critics of air pollution as enemies of human progress.[11]

Rand's Objectivist movement disintegrated in the late 1960s; by that time Rand had driven off or excommunicated the greater part of her inner circle. In truth, it must be said that Rand was never a libertarian. She was too intolerant of others' preferences for that. Also, her readiness to mount an anticommunist crusade brought her much too close to endorsing a "statist" foreign pol-

*For libertarians, Rand's two most important novels are *The Fountainhead* (1943) and *Atlas Shrugged* (1957). Rand's philosophy is not taken seriously by very many philosophers (a fact that to Rand is proof of the collectivist conspiracy). A notable exception is Hazel Barnes, who discusses Rand's doctrine of egoism in *An Existentialist Ethics* (Chicago: University of Chicago Press, 1967).

icy. Nevertheless, Rand's unqualified support of laissez-faire capitalism and her dire warnings against the collectivist ethic were clearly in line with libertarian concerns. Her devotees had little difficulty making their way from Objectivism to libertarianism.

If any one person deserves to be called the founder of the modern libertarian movement, that person is Murray Rothbard. Rothbard is an economist trained in the method of the Austrian school by Ludwig von Mises, an early critic of the Keynesian revolution and a long-time opponent of socialism.* Like his mentor, Rothbard is convinced of the technical superiority of the free-market economy and is devoted to the ideal of a market society. Well versed in the antistatist tradition, he is a prolific author and a tireless organizer. He has been a zealot on behalf of the libertarian cause for more than three decades.

Rothbard is perhaps a model of the secular intellectual who has discovered a new faith. In one place he describes his acceptance of the libertarian "creed" in terms reminiscent of a religious conversion experience. "When I became a libertarian," he writes, ". . . the thrill of discovery of this hidden truth, a truth as vital to mankind as the nature of liberty and justice, was so great that it was impossible for me to conceive—and still difficult for me to understand—how anyone, *once* perceiving this great truth, could possibly defect from or abandon it."[12] Ironically, Rothbard him-

---

*The libertarian approach to economics is strongly influenced by the teachings of the Austrian school. The Austrian method is associated with the legacy of Carl Menger, one of the pioneers of the marginalist revolution of the 1870s. Menger's ideas were developed and promulgated by his students Eugen von Böhm-Bawerk and Friedrich von Wieser at the University of Vienna. Their work was carried on in Vienna and later in America by Ludwig von Mises, the teacher of both Friedrich Hayek and Murray Rothbard. The Austrian school has not been a potent force in the field of economics for more than half a century, but an attempted revival is now being encouraged by the libertarian movement. The libertarian Institute for Humane Studies in Menlo Park, California, has published a series of works describing Austrian theory and its place in the history of economic thought. Included are *The Economic Point of View*, by Israel Kirzner (a leader of the Austrian revival); *New Directions in Austrian Economics*, edited by Louis Spadaro (past director of the Institute for Humane Studies); and *The Foundations of Modern Austrian Economics*, edited by Edwin G. Dolan.

self found the religious analogy convenient. In his keynote address to the 1977 Libertarian party convention, he described becoming a libertarian as a two-stage "conversion."

> The first conversion is what we might call the "baptism of reason"—the moment or moments when the person becomes convinced that liberty is the best, the only just, social system for mankind. He or she realizes that liberty is the true, the good, and the beautiful. . . . To be truly "born again," the libertarian must experience what we might call a second baptism, the "baptism of will." That is, he must be driven by his rational insight to dedicate himself to the mighty goal of bringing about the victory of liberty, of libertarian principles, in the real world. He must set out to transform reality in accordance with his ideal vision.[13]

The true, the good, and the beautiful: here indeed is a rock on which to build a church, or at the least a militant sect of true believers. But Rothbard was certainly not the only libertarian prophet. Once a member of Rand's inner circle, he had to compete with Rand herself and a host of lesser lights in order to win a following. Rothbard was unusual in that he performed much of his missionary work among the enemy. In the 1960s, when Rand was denouncing the youth rebellion as an "anti-industrial revolution," Rothbard dreamed of building an alliance between Nock's remnant and the antiwar, antiestablishment New Left. Writing in *Ramparts* in 1968, he drew a parallel between the contemporary antiwar movement and the isolationist Old Right of the 1940s and early 1950s, which had also opposed conscription, militarism, and American "imperialist aggression" (in Korea).[14]

The coalition of left and right that Rothbard hoped for never materialized. He did, however, manage to convert Barry Goldwater's former aid Karl Hess to libertarianism, and helped bring about a schism in the conservative Young Americans for Freedom, which split over the war issue in 1969; afterward, dissident YAFers broke away to form the libertarian Society for Individual Liberty. In 1969 Rothbard made a first attempt to bring all shades of libertarian opinion together in the Radical Libertarian Alliance. The attempt was less than successful. Jerome Tuccille, another Goldwater conservative converted to libertarianism, writes that the RLA "comprised a multifaceted assortment worthy of inclusion in anybody's gallery of American oddities." It seems that most members of Rothbard's would-be alliance were devotees of Rand. Among the others, according to Tuccille, were

> radical entrepreneurs who wanted to remake the United States into a gigantic shopping center owned and managed by a single real estate concern, thereby eliminating the functions of the United States government; libertarian royalists who thought wealthy individualists should buy up large tracts of land and turn them into fiefdoms under a libertarian code of justice; anarcho–Minute Men who wanted to take to the mountains à la Che Guevara and organize a revolutionary guerrilla movement for intransigent free enterprisers; radical reformists who favored moving all the libertarians in the country into a single state, Nevada or Wyoming perhaps, and taking over the political structure through the electoral process.[15]

Still others, Tuccille reports, wanted to colonize the moon or establish a libertarian Atlantis on the ocean bottom. A disastrous convention held in the fall of 1969 convinced Rothbard that his attempt to create a unified movement was premature.

The libertarian movement finally managed to coalesce by entering politics. It might never have done so had it not been for Richard Nixon. It was Nixon's decision to impose wage and price controls in 1971 that led a handful of renegade Young Republicans to float the idea of launching a new political party. At their instigation, the Libertarian party held its first convention early in 1972. Their meeting was plagued by the same divisions that had wrecked the Radical Libertarian Alliance; nevertheless, the party organizers managed to hammer out a platform and send the delegates home committed to a slate of candidates. Heading their presidential ticket was John Hospers, chairman of the philosophy department at the University of Southern California and the author of a book on libertarianism.[16] Hospers'

name appeared on the ballot in only two states, and he recorded a
mere 5,000 popular votes; however, a Republican elector from
Virginia, Roger MacBride, broke ranks with his party to cast his
electoral college ballot for Hospers. In 1976 MacBride would be
the Libertarian candidate for president.

Initially the Libertarian party was dominated by people who
had come to libertarianism by way of Rand's Objectivism. Rothbard, discouraged by his experience with the Radical Libertarian
Alliance, was at first wary of the party. It was not long, however, before he was enlisted as a top political strategist. Under his
influence the party became a more radical critic of the state and at
the same time a more professionally minded political organization. Rothbard intended to win elections. He came to see the
party as a vehicle for creating the new coalition in American
politics that he had long hoped to establish.

In 1976 the Libertarian party was on the ballot in thirty-two
states and its presidential candidate amassed almost 175,000
votes. In the off-year elections of 1978 the party polled over one
million votes nationwide in a variety of state and local contests.
In Alaska that year the voters sent a Libertarian to the state
legislature. In California's gubernatorial contest, corporation
lawyer Ed Clark, who was destined to become the party's 1980
presidential nominee, won nearly 400,000 votes, the best showing for a third-party candidate in California in nearly three decades. The libertarian presence was suddenly noticeable.

Libertarianism received new intellectual respectability with the
publication of Robert Nozick's *Anarchy, State, and Utopia* in
1974. Nozick, a Harvard philosopher, took seriously the arguments concerning state and society put forward by the likes of
Rand and Rothbard. Responding to these thinkers and to others
outside the libertarian camp, most notably his colleague John
Rawls, Nozick advanced a rights-oriented defense of the minimal state that established libertarian political theory as a serious
alternative, at least in academic discourse.

Around the same time industrialist Charles Koch began to
provide the libertarian cause with a more tangible form of support. Koch, a former member of the John Birch Society, had

been converted to libertarianism by the social and economic writings of Rothbard's teacher Ludwig von Mises. As heir to the fourth largest family-owned business in the nation (Koch Industries, an oil-based conglomerate), Koch possessed the wherewithal to fund a series of libertarian organizations that he helped set up after the 1976 election. Chief among these enterprises are the Cato Institute, a public policy research foundation in San Francisco budgeted at over $1 million a year; the Students for a Libertarian Society, a largely ineffective effort to organize the campuses; the *Libertarian Review,* a monthly magazine designed to serve the movement; *Inquiry,* a semimonthly magazine published by the Cato Institute and designed to appeal to a broad audience (*Inquiry* is thoroughly antistatist but not dogmatically libertarian and regularly features well-known writers on the political left, such as Nat Hentoff and Noam Chomsky)*; the Institute for Humane Studies, a center for libertarian scholarship located in Menlo Park, California; and the Council for a Competitive Economy, a businessmen's group based in Washington, D.C., intended as a libertarian alternative to the National Association of Manufacturers. While an exact figure is not available, it is estimated that Koch has already spent several million dollars to promote libertarianism.[17] In 1980 Koch's brother David was the Libertarian party's candidate for vice-president. He gained his place on the ticket by promising to contribute several hundred thousand dollars to the campaign.[18]

Buoyed by the 1978 returns, Libertarian party officials predicted an even stronger showing in 1980. Though by no means hoping for victory, they looked forward to winning between 2 and 4 percent of the total vote, enough to give the new party high visibility in an electoral contest often decided by a slim margin. In light of these expectations, the party's actual showing of less than 1 percent, though still more than a million votes, must be seen as a disappointment. Why in a year marked by the

---

*That the likes of Hentoff and Chomsky can be found in the pages of *Inquiry* suggests the attractiveness of libertarian antistatism to the American left. It also serves to underscore the fact that although the sectarian libertarian political movement originates on the right, the appeal of libertarianism is much broader.

voters' apparent rejection of the "more is better" philosophy of government did the libertarians score no better than they did?

No doubt to ask the question is in part to answer it. In an election in which Big Government was attacked from all sides, the libertarian candidate could hardly claim a monopoly on virtue. Beyond the obvious, however, lies an important distinction to be made in the ideological character of the 1980 election. The rhetoric may have been generally antistatist, but the themes that carried the day were not those dearest to the libertarians.

By far the most prominent ideological force in the 1980 election was the coalition of conservative political action committees, single-interest lobbies, and evangelical groups that together make up the New Right.[19]* Superficially, the New Right groups and the libertarians appear to have much in common. Both sing hymns to the free market and regard government regulation as economic heresy. Both vehemently condemn the welfare state and rampant "egalitarianism." But while libertarians see the state itself as inherently evil, a real or potential violator of individual rights, the New Right is more than willing to use the power of the state for ends it thinks proper. Those ends include the legislation of morality (in regard to abortion, homosexuality, and other "family" issues) and massive defense spending coupled with an aggressive foreign policy.[20] The Moral Majority, Inc., and the American Security Council are separated from the Libertarian party by an unbridgeable ideological abyss.

The partisan "warfare" that goes on between libertarians and conservatives may best be described as a blood feud. In *Ramparts* Rothbard complained that the rise of the "new right" in the 1950s—he means the global anticommunism of the *National Review* crowd—signaled the "capture" of America's right wing by "elitists and devotees of the European conservative ideals of

*This is not to say that the election marked a swing to the right on the part of the American public. Walter Dean Burnham's analysis of the data suggests that this was not the case, but rather an instance of "throwing the rascals out." See Burnham's essay "The 1980 Earthquake: Realignment, Reaction, or What?" in *The Hidden Election,* ed. Thomas Ferguson and Joel Rogers (New York: Pantheon Books, 1981), pp. 109–10.

order and militarism." Unlike the old-time conservatives, who were really old-time (nineteenth-century) liberals, these new conservatives were statists who wished to coerce "morality" and suppress "sedition."[21] Shortly after the *Ramparts* piece appeared, Frank Meyer asked in the pages of the *National Review* whether Rothbard's doctrine was called libertarianism or libertinism, commenting that Rothbard's politics had become "indistinguishable from that of SDS."[22] More recently Ernest van den Haag has criticized the libertarian movement for naively objecting "not just to specific laws, but to legislation, to the authority of the state, and its coercive power, *per se*," and for having "consistently taken extreme leftist positions" on issues of national defense and foreign policy.[23]

This dispute between self-styled conservatives and libertarians illuminates the ambivalence of the American right, which despite European borrowings is still firmly rooted in the Lockean consensus.[24] Even the "conservative" who is an ardent statist on military matters turns out to be a libertarian free enterpriser when it comes to managing the economy. For their part, libertarians invoke the Old Right against the new and newer rights of the 1950s and the 1970s in order to divorce their laissez-faire economics from cold-war militarism and domestic moralism. It is precisely because libertarians and conservatives share so much common ground that their mutual hostility is so intense.

Antistatism, individualism, capitalism, and isolationism have deep roots in the American psyche. Discounting the electoral failures of the Libertarian party, for the odds are always stacked against third parties in American politics, it is surprising that libertarianism has not met with a better reception. In the final analysis, libertarianism fails with the many for the same reason it succeeds with the few. As a reaffirmation of familiar themes, it elevates the stuff of everyday life to the level of dogma. The party of principle, as libertarians bill themselves, is intolerant of those it considers unprincipled. Converts are welcome, but there is no compromise possible with those who refuse to accept the libertarian creed. Surely this is no way to develop a mass following.

Yet the libertarians are undaunted. They believe in the effectiveness of political education and boast that once their principles are understood, libertarianism will become irresistible. Their optimism is testimony to their faith in the power of ideas and the rightness of their own convictions. From the libertarian point of view, once enlightened, only a genuinely evil person—one who hopes to profit from the ignorance of others by gaining power over them—will continue in opposition. History may have long favored statists, but their days are numbered. The contest between liberty and power, understood as a struggle between good and evil, admits of only one conclusion. In Rothbard's words,

> libertarianism will win eventually because it and only it is compatible with the nature of man and of the world. Only liberty can achieve man's prosperity, fulfillment, and happiness. In short, libertarianism will win because it is true, because it is the correct policy for mankind, and truth will eventually win out.[25]

Thus historical politics gives way to a secular eschatology. In the future looms a political Armageddon, and beyond it a libertarian millennium.

3

Libertarianism and the Crisis of Public Authority

I believe the single most remarkable fact at the present time in the West is neither technological nor economic, but political: the waning of the historic political community, the widening sense of the obsolescence of politics as a civilized pursuit, even as a habit of mind.

—ROBERT NISBET, *Twilight of Authority*

IF the libertarians may be taken at their word, many among them believe that the millennium is fast approaching. Edward H. Crane III, a Libertarian party official and director of the Cato Institute, told a reporter before the 1980 presidential election that he fully expected to see the inauguration of a Libertarian president in his lifetime.[1] Libertarian theorist Murray Rothbard has expressed his personal optimism somewhat more colorfully in *For a New Liberty*, subtitled *The Libertarian Manifesto*. (Rothbard, who fancies himself at the heart of a revolutionary movement, enjoys being referred to as the Karl Marx of libertarianism.) "I am convinced," he writes, "that the dark night of tyranny is ending, and that a new dawn of liberty in now at hand."[2] Rothbard's optimism flows from his perception of what he describes as a "crisis situation" confronting the modern state. His understanding of this "crisis" derives less from an examination of current events than from a crude theory of history that might well qualify as an inverse Marxism. According to Rothbard, not capitalism but socialism (or, more broadly, statism) will eventually collapse under the weight of its own internal contradiction.

35

Rothbard understands history to be progressive; that progress, however, is said to have begun only two centuries ago. From Rothbard's libertarian perspective, tyranny was the condition of human existence from the dawn of civilization until the latter part of the eighteenth century. At this crucial juncture advances in philosophy and technology gave humankind the possibility of freedom. Rothbard credits classical liberalism and the Industrial Revolution with creating the intellectual means and objective conditions necessary for a restructuring of the political world. Tyranny had been universal from the earliest times, largely for want of an alternative; "the masses knew no better, had never experienced a better system, and hence could be induced to keep serving as beasts of burden for their lords." In a dramatic break with the past (Rothbard calls it a "great leap in history"), classical liberalism armed Western peoples with the idea of liberty. There followed a series of "cataclysmic revolutions" in America and in France that "blasted loose the Old Order and the old ruling classes" and won at least a partial victory for individual freedom and laissez-faire. Equally important, these political revolutions made possible the Industrial Revolution, and industrial technology brought an end to the peasant economy of the ancien régime, which had long condemned the masses to bare subsistence. Here lies the political significance of the Industrial Revolution: in the rising standard of living it made possible and the consequent revolution of rising expectations. Ultimately it is in this psychological bedrock and not in any abstract love of liberty that Rothbard anchors his hopes. The clock cannot be turned back to a preindustrial age, he contends, because the masses would never permit "such a drastic reversal of their expectations for a rising standard of living." Triumphantly he announces that "we are stuck with the industrial age, whether we like it or not." And to him this means we are "stuck" with laissez-faire capitalism, because "*only* freedom and a free market can run an industrial economy."[3]

As far as Rothbard is concerned, one thing is certain, whether or not the masses ever grasp the essentials of libertarianism: statism must fail because it violates the indisputable truths of economic science. And, as Rothbard sees it, time is running out for the state. His economism of the right (one is tempted to say economic determinism) posits the imminent collapse of state-controlled (i.e., state-disrupted) economies around the world. Yet if all Rothbard claims is true, how is it that statism has survived for so long? Rothbard has an answer. He explains that the modern state could "wreak its depredations" on the economy through planning, controls, high taxes, and inflation without causing "clear and *evident* crises and dislocations" because

> the free market industrialization of the nineteenth century had created a vast cushion of "fat" in the economy against such depredations. But now statism has advanced so far and been in power so long that the cushion is worn thin; as [Ludwig von] Mises pointed out as long ago as the 1940s, the "reserve fund" created by laissez-faire has been "exhausted." So that now, whatever the government does brings about an instant negative feedback—ill effects that are evident to all, even to many of the most ardent apologists for statism.[4]

Although he insists that the present crisis exists worldwide, Rothbard believes it is particularly acute in the United States. He claims that in the early 1970s the nation entered a "permanent crisis situation" marked by high inflation, fiscal instability, and growing citizen discontent. He is cheered by the course of events. With the consequences of statism clearly exposed, the conditions are ripe for the triumph of his cause. "All that is needed is a growing and vibrant libertarian movement to explain the systemic crisis and to point out the libertarian path out of our government-created morass."[5]

There is more ideology than economics in Rothbard's libertarian manifesto, or perhaps it is an instance of economics as ideology. Yet his perception of a crisis situation of sorts in American politics ought not to be lightly dismissed. Certainly one cannot help thinking something is amiss when politicians campaign for office, even at the highest levels of government, as critics of the very institutions they seek to control. With their eyes fixed on public opinion polls, many observers comment that citizen discontent signals a real threat to the legitimacy of the state. There is a growing consensus among scholars and pundits alike that government in America has promised more than it can deliver, much to the damage of its own credibility. Widely perceived as ineffective and perhaps even illegitimate, the state confronts what can be called a crisis of public authority.

A noted scholar who has argued this case is Samuel Huntington, an authority on American political development. In "The Democratic Distemper," an essay initially written for the Trilateral Commission, Huntington attributes the current crisis to the political mobilization of the 1960s. He argues that new political actors (minorities, women, the young) with new demands on the system were effectively coopted by means of new government programs; this additional load, however, strained public resources and undermined the capacity of government to execute its own policies. In short, the system was "overloaded." The legacy of this period, according to Huntington, is a government that cannot meet public expectations and in consequence cannot govern effectively.

Huntington's essay has an essentially conservative purpose. Having diagnosed the problem as resulting from an "excess of democracy," he sees no solution but to rein in the democratic process.[6] Nevertheless, his argument serves to establish the crisis of public authority as in large measure a reaction against the politics and programs of the 1960s. Whether or not the variety of social welfare policies enacted in that decade overloaded the state, it is clear they engendered a great deal of resentment. As Huntington notes, the state effectively attempted to expand its constituency by reaching out to groups formerly excluded from the political process or whose status was marginal; but in doing so it not only raised their expectations, it angered many among its traditional constituents, no small number of whom felt threatened by the new policies.

The crisis of public authority, then, has its immediate origin in the increasingly bitter political contest over the use of limited public resources. At a deeper level, however, the crisis originates in the structure of American politics that emerged after the New

Deal. The case for an inherent crisis has been made most force-fully by Theodore J. Lowi in his study of postwar politics, *The End of Liberalism*. Lowi argues that the newly expanded state was a timid creature, eager to do good but wary of seeming too powerful. Like most Americans, the architects of the positive state were uneasy with the concept of power, and so they sought a formula that would avoid concentrating power in the organs of government. They struck upon the course of investing private interests with public authority, thereby diffusing power and at the same time deemphasizing the role of government. To put that another way, public policy was allowed to originate with private groups (organized interests) which enjoyed institu-tionalized access to government. Each "clientele" group could plug into government through a specialized bureaucratic appa-ratus. This system was justified by the belief that the public interest would be served through the satisfaction of the variety of private interests. The role of the state was seen to be one of "insuring access to the most effectively organized, and of ratify-ing the agreements and adjustments worked out among the com-peting leaders."[7]

Lowi calls this ersatz political theory underlying the operation of the modern American state "interest group liberalism." (The name derives from the marriage of pluralist political assumptions regarding groups and the liberal conception of the public good as the sum of individual preferences.) He argues that the effect of interest group liberalism as a system of politics is automatically to legitimate almost any demand made on government. There are simply no grounds for denying the claim of any organized interest so long as the group abides by the rules of the game, and no standards exist by which to evaluate the claim of any one group in competition with others. This does not mean, of course, that all claims receive equal attention; the unorganized and the poorly organized may go unheard altogether. In this respect the system creates and perpetuates privilege. At the same time, interest group liberalism invites the systemic "overload" of which Huntington complains. Indeed, with no lid on the pork barrel, interest group liberalism may have made such an overload inevitable.

Lowi makes the point that as a public philosophy interest group liberalism is flawed precisely because it leaves us unable to distinguish the public good from private interests. One consequence is public cynicism. Another is the marked inability of government to plan, because public policy is never more than a patchwork garment tailored to the disparate needs of a broad clientele. And so an uncomfortable paradox develops: as the scope of government activity widens in response to political pressures, the purposes for which the state acts become less coherent and less intelligible. Ironically this paradox has its roots in the liberal distrust of power. Ultimately the crisis of public authority can be recognized as the identity crisis of the liberal democratic state.

Sooner or later this crisis must be resolved. It is prolonged at the expense of government's effectiveness, and none of the groups now accustomed to the exercise of public power on their behalf will tolerate the inconvenience indefinitely. The resultant strain on our political economy and the processes of social accommodation is too great. Visions of just how the crisis will be resolved vary with the perspective of the seer. The view on the left, as represented by political sociologist Alan Wolfe, is of the future as a contest between large corporate interests and popular democracy for control of the state. Wolfe writes that "the major political issues will not take place within the parameters of liberal democracy but over them."[8] On the right, meanwhile, the likes of Samuel Huntington and sociologist Robert Nisbet foresee the collapse of all authority—which means either chaos or a totalitarianism born of chaos—if the forces of democracy are not restrained. Their argument is that the liberal state can survive only if we ask less of it.[9]

What unites such political antagonists as Wolfe and Huntington, despite their obvious differences, is their assumption that the public interest can be discovered and used as a compass to chart a way clear of the present crisis. From the libertarian point of view, however, this assumption is groundless. As far as the libertarian observer is concerned, there is no "public interest" because there is no "public." To speak of society or of the public as if these words referred to living entities with wants and needs of their own is to commit a grave methodological error. Collectivities, the libertarian instructs, do not have interests; only individuals do. Of course, individuals may make common cause with one another to secure their interests, but this alliance does not create a group interest independent of the ends sought by its members. To reason otherwise is to commit the collectivist fallacy. The consequence of such reasoning (and, of course, from the libertarian perspective, the intended consequence) is tyranny: those who control the state would justify their dominion over others by enforcing ends of their own choosing in the name of the common good.

Once again libertarianism echoes themes close to the center of the American political tradition. It appeals, perhaps unaware, to the Madisonian distrust of faction which reappears episodically throughout our history as the populist fear of special privilege. Madison believed that each faction in its pursuit of privilege and power would naturally serve as a check on the others. In a variation on Madison's logic, interest group liberalism would neutralize privilege by making it universal. Americans have always been wary of selfish interests masquerading as the general interest; yet mainstream American politics has never rejected the concept of a general interest. It was the general interest Madison sought to protect from the ills of faction. With similar intent, interest group liberalism, which may be thought to have institutionalized faction, is believed to promote the common good by serving the discrete needs of multitudinous interests. Generally in the American political culture political power is distrusted but not despised; the public interest is an ambiguous yet viable concept.

Libertarianism is distinguished by its extreme hostility toward political power and its refusal to consider the public interest anything but a cruel hoax. Libertarians define power as coercion or the threat of coercion. To exercise political power, then, is to employ the coercive potential of the state against the citizenry. In Rothbard's terms, the state is necessarily an aggressor. By implication, political power is incompatible with liberty. This fatal objection is deemed no less conclusive when it is applied to the democratic state. In the lesson of a parable borrowed from Herbert Spencer, Robert Nozick explains that a man ruled by others against his will, whose life and property are under their control, is no less a slave because he has the vote and may periodically "choose" his masters.[10] Who can deny that even in a democracy, legitimated by popular elections, most if not all persons at least some of the time will be forced to endure government policies they strongly oppose? Libertarians argue that the fact of majority rule, when and where it is a fact, cannot disguise the coercive nature of political power. As Rothbard cynically observes, "the lynch mob, too, is a majority in its own domain."[11] Given that political power, under even the most favorable circumstances, is incompatible with liberty, it follows that if we wish to maximize the latter we should as much as possible avoid use of the former. This is the rationale behind the Libertarian party platform, which, unlike most party platforms, lists the things government should *not* do. In a seeming contradiction, the libertarians are running a political campaign to abolish politics.

The abolition of politics is the libertarians' solution to the crisis of public authority. Their idea is to replace government with the market wherever possible. Thus the state is not to provide any goods or services that can be secured from private entrepreneurs. Libertarians are confident that everything from garbage collection and the provision of municipal services to education and space exploration lies within the competence of the free market. Nor is the state to interfere in the operation of the market. Buyers and sellers are assumed to be capable of looking after their own affairs. Libertarians are aware that practicality is an issue. Can such vital services as fire protection be restricted to subscribers without jeopardizing everyone's safety? And what will become of those persons who cannot afford the going rates for needed services? In regard to the first question, libertarians see no problem. They are not bothered by the image of firefighters hosing down a client's home while a neighbor's house burns to the ground. The foolish neighbor must live with the consequences of his parsimony (he, too, should have subscribed to the fire company). As to the second question, libertarians respond that eager entrepreneurs are likely to develop a range of services in all areas priced to meet market demand. Competitive pricing will be no less true of fire protection and like services than it is for tennis sneakers and other widely available consumer goods. To the state is left the task of securing the market against enemies foreign and domestic (i.e., warring states and thieves) and of guaranteeing the enforcement of contracts through its court system.

The most radical libertarians, who favor abolishing the state altogether, believe that the principle of laissez-faire may equally well be applied to police protection and the administration of justice. The ultimate aim of these "anarchocapitalists" is the creation of a stateless society governed only by the economic laws of the marketplace. Anarchocapitalism is the ultimate expression of the libertarian retreat from politics. Its advocates conceive of society as nothing more than a loose collection of autonomous individuals, a virtual Lockean state of nature. The familiar notion of the public is conceptually obliterated, leaving no trace of a political community and no vestige of a common purpose save that degree of cooperation required to achieve the disparate ends of intensely private individuals. As if to underscore this point, Murray Rothbard's portrait of the stateless society discards all symbols of the public dimension to collective life; even the streets and highways are privately owned, to be traversed at the owner's discretion (and, no doubt, for a fee). In the absence of a political community, the rights of property replace the rights of citizenship. The right of free speech, for example, becomes in Rothbard's terms "the property right to hire an assembly hall from the owners, or to own one oneself."[12] In the anarchocapitalist world the individual owes allegiance to no one; the only obligation one has is to honor one's contracts.

A critic might argue that the libertarians would abolish political power only to establish the tyranny of economic power. Indeed, persons of little or no property appear to have few if any "rights" in a libertarian society. Nor is it clear that all would enjoy real liberty. While there is to be little or no coercion by the state, what need is there of coercive measures when one person's poverty will virtually compel him "voluntarily" to accept any condition of employment, however oppressive, simply to ensure his survival? Yet even this "worst case" example fails to impress libertarian theorists. Their position is best represented by Friedrich Hayek, who chooses precisely this example to make his point.

> Even if the threat of starvation to me and perhaps to my family impels me to accept a distasteful job at a very low wage, even if I am "at the mercy" of the only man willing to employ me, I am not coerced by him or anybody else. So long as the act that placed me in my predicament is not aimed at making me do or not do specific things, so long as the intent of the act that harms me is not to make me serve another person's ends, its effect on my freedom is not entirely different from that of any natural calamity—a fire or a flood that destroys my home or an accident that injures my health.[13]

It is Hayek's contention, generally shared by libertarian thinkers, that the force of circumstance is not the moral equivalent of human coercion; liberty is lost only when an identifiable oppressor works his will on some particular victim or victims. Thus a market economy devoid of force and fraud (in which participation is, by definition, voluntary) may impose severe constraints on individuals but cannot be said to abridge anyone's liberty. Like a natural disaster, a calamitous market outcome is impersonal; though the product of human agency, the unfortunate result is unintended. This emphasis on intention allows Hayek to ignore the possibility of systemic bias inherent in the structure of market relations. Since one's location in the market system is merely fortuitous, the lack of meaningful options available to any given person or class of persons is irrelevant from the standpoint of liberty. Our freedom, Hayek observes, "does not ensure us any particular opportunities, but leaves it to us to decide what use we shall make of the circumstances in which we find ourselves." Freedom, though a necessary condition for the pursuit of happiness, cannot guarantee the result. "Above all," Hayek cautions, "we must recognize that we may be free and yet miserable."[14]

To be free and yet miserable seems cold comfort; indeed, if the unfortunate victims of circumstance were given the choice between politically amending market outcomes and preserving their freedom (and thus perpetuating their misery), there can be little doubt as to how they would vote. Fortunately for the cause of liberty, libertarians foresee little actual misery once the heavy hand of government has been lifted from the market. As a matter of fact, economic conditions are expected to improve tremendously. So highly do libertarians praise the efficiency and productivity of the market that at times it seems they value liberty less for its own sake than for the degree of material wealth it makes possible.[15] Of course, this wealth will not be shared equally, and there is always a danger to property in the feelings of resentment inspired by inequality. Envious persons might well become thieves, or possibly revolutionaries. That is why even anarchocapitalists posit a need for some kind of police agency.

The emphasis libertarians place on the opposition of liberty and political power tends to obscure the role of authority in their worldview. Clearly, political authority stands condemned by virtue of its association with the coercive power of the state. The authority exercised in private relationships, however—in the relationship between employer and employee, for instance—meets no objection. Here authority is understood to be grounded in the express consent of the employee, who is free to withdraw his consent (i.e., to resign) at any time. Even in the worst case situation, where the individual must choose between oppressive conditions of employment and starvation, his or her freedom is complete: though the individual may rightly complain of being compelled by circumstance, the salient point is that no one forces him or her to accept the job. However strongly felt by the employee, the authority of the boss is not dominion.

The pure formalism of this argument reveals a curious insensitivity to the use of private authority as a means of social control. Comparing public and private authority, we might well ask of the libertarians: When the price of exercising one's freedom is terribly high, what practical difference is there between the commands of the state and those issued by one's employer? Will disagreeable commands from the latter seem any less offensive than those that have a political origin? Though admittedly the circumstances are not identical, telling disgruntled employees that they are always free to leave their jobs seems no different in principle from telling political dissidents that they are free to emigrate. In either case freedom affords little or no protection against the demand for conformity. The problem with the libertarian argument is that *negative* liberty, defined as the absence of coercion, cannot guarantee individual autonomy, or *positive* liberty, the freedom to act and to choose one's actions independently.[16] Though autonomy may be jeopardized by the use of force, its opposite is not coercion but dependency. The tension between negative liberty and autonomy would not occur if each individual were self-sufficient, for then there would be no effective economic sanction against nonconformity. But in a modern corporate economy, where ownership of the means of production is concentrated within a narrow social stratum and most persons must sell their labor in order to live, the great majority of persons will find their autonomy gravely circumscribed.

Concern for individual autonomy has been a staple feature of Anglo-American political thought. The classical republican theorists of the seventeenth century were prepared to deny the privileges of citizenship to any person who served in the employ of another, because economic dependency was believed to subvert the free and independent judgment required of a citizen; the servant was presumed to be his master's tool.[17] Later, after the triumph of republicanism, conservatives used this argument to oppose extension of the franchise to the working class.[18] Nineteenth-century electoral reforms (prominent among them the secret ballot) were designed to neutralize the lack of autonomy in the voter's everday life by providing anonymity on election day. In short, as the Anglo-American political tradition was gradually democratized, the attempt was made to reconcile the individual's economic and political identities. It is economic man that must contend with circumstance and may find his autonomy limited by his situation. The citizen, on the other hand, is guaranteed a certain measure of autonomy by the state.

The autonomy of the citizen is protected in the main by constitutional provisions safeguarding the exercise of certain rights (First Amendment freedoms, for example). While the United States Constitution expressly restricts only public authority in this regard, prohibiting government from violating the protected rights, Congress and the courts have seen fit on several occasions to extend these restrictions to private authority as well. Such is the confusion between the rights of property and the rights of citizenship in our constitutional tradition that these decisions have most recently been based on the federal government's power to regulate interstate commerce, or on a finding of "substantial" state involvement in an otherwise private act. So it is that privately owned restaurants open to the general public may not refuse black patrons for fear of disrupting the flow of interstate commerce, and businesses holding government contracts may not discriminate against racial minorities or women because their action would attach to the state.[19]

A more compelling and less circuitous argument on behalf of the rights of citizenship was advanced a century ago by Justice John Marshall Harlan in his dissenting opinion to the Civil Rights Cases of 1883. A Supreme Court majority had voted to strike down a federal antidiscrimination statute passed by the Reconstruction Congress. The law mandated equal treatment for blacks at taverns, inns, and places of public amusement. Harlan defended the statute by arguing that where private property assumes a public character, the rights of citizenship, including the right of equal access to public places, must prevail over the property rights of the owner.*

*Harlan wrote:

> I am of the opinion that [racial] discrimination practised by corporations and individuals in the exercise of their public or quasi-public functions is a badge of servitude the imposition of which Congress may prevent under its power, by appropriate legislation, to enforce the [Thirteenth Amendment]. . . . In every material sense applicable to the practical enforcement of the Fourteenth Amendment [granting citizenship to the former slaves], railroad corporations, keepers of inns, and managers of places of public amusement are agents or instrumentalities of the State, because they are charged with duties to the public, and are amenable, in respect of their duties and functions, to governmental regulation. [109 U.S. 3, 3 S.Ct. 18, 27 L. Ed. 835 (1883)]

To be sure, even with so generous an interpretation as Harlan's, the rights of citizenship cannot fully compensate an individual for the lack of autonomy in his or her private life. At best these rights create a "public space" in which some of the effects of inequality and economic dependency are rendered inconsequential. Within this limited space citizens confront one another as equals.[20]

This narrow sphere of equality is threatened by the libertarian assault on the political. To abolish politics, as the libertarians would have us do, is to commit the individual to the world of circumstance where men and women may be formally free but have little or no control over their own lives. This prospect fails to disturb libertarian theorists because they correctly perceive that there is no way to preserve a measure of autonomy for all without intruding on the property rights of some. Having made the protection of property tantamount to the preservation of freedom, their system admits no justification for abridging the prerogatives of ownership.

If libertarians seem unmindful of the problem of autonomy, perhaps it is because they do not consider it an issue of any great importance. After all, economic interdependence encouraged by the division of labor is a characteristic feature of the free market. Absent a showing of force or fraud, the social consequences of interdependence are morally neutral. Men and women remain free, however limited the use they can make of their freedom.

Of far greater interest to libertarians is the expression of individuality through one's choice of a lifestyle. Individualism is a familiar theme with broad appeal in the American political culture. The libertarian approach to individualism, which merges personal and property rights, suits perfectly the modern consumer society, where "you are what you own." Moreover, it reflects a concept of the self and of self-fulfillment already widespread in the United States. The pursuit of happiness has become the pursuit of pleasure. And while happiness has always proved an elusive goal, pleasure can assume the more concrete form of possessions and the perquisites of wealth. In this context the libertarian critique of victimless crimes becomes an assertion of the right of every consumer to the lifestyle he or she can afford.

To paraphrase Robert Nozick, individualism means that capitalist acts among consenting adults are not to be interfered with.

So blatantly materialistic a view of what Peter Clecak has admiringly termed "America's quest for the ideal self" risks turning self-fulfillment into mere self-indulgence.[21] On this premise, libertarianism invites us to forget politics in an orgy of hedonism. It should come as no surprise to find the *Libertarian Review* featuring an article in praise of the "me decade" of the 1970s.[22] Any preoccupation with the self, whatever its ideological orientation, complements the libertarian retreat from politics. As the historian and social critic Christopher Lasch observes of the self-awareness movement, it betrays a revulsion against politics—"revulsion, that is, against the hope of using politics as an instrument of social change." If Lasch is correct, the cult of self-awareness extolled by the *Review* is but one symptom of a dying culture—the bourgeois culture of competitive individualism, "which in its decadence has carried the logic of individualism to the extreme of a war of all against all, the pursuit of happiness to the dead end of a narcissistic preoccupation with the self."[23] From this perspective, libertarianism, as a form of antipolitics in harmony with the anomic individualism of our times, is less a response to the crisis of public authority than a symptom of that crisis and of the deeper societal malaise that lies behind it.

4

The Philosophic Roots
of Radical Libertarianism

To understand Political Power right, and derive it from its original, we must consider what State all Men are naturally in, and
that is, *a State of perfect Freedom* to order their Actions as they
think fit, within the bounds of the Law of Nature, without
asking leave, or depending upon the Will of any other man.
—JOHN LOCKE, *The Second Treatise of Government*

LIBERTARIAN political thought is composed of two strands.
The first, perhaps best represented by Harvard philosopher
Robert Nozick, attempts to reinvigorate the idea of the night-
watchman state by denying the moral legitimacy of any more
expansive concept of government. The second strand, more radical in content than the first, rejects even the minimal state allowed by Nozick and embraces a variety of anarchism, which its
proponents call anarchocapitalism.

It is not difficult to understand why some libertarians are
drawn to anarchism. Having defined liberty as the absence of
coercion and finding the exercise of political power to be the
primary instance of coercion, they logically conclude that liberty
and government are incompatible. Defenders of the minimal
state differ only in asserting that a small degree of personal liberty must be surrendered to government in exchange for the guaranteed security of life and property. Indeed, were it not for the
perception of human nature shared with Thomas Hobbes, that
human beings require "a common Power to keep them in awe,"

the architects of classical liberalism from whom the libertarians descend would have had no use for the state whatsoever. Anarchocapitalists have merely recalculated the utility of government to discover that the costs far outweigh the benefits.

The words "anarchism" and "liberalism" do not usually occur together. Nineteenth-century liberals may have praised the "anarchy" of the marketplace in their defense of unbridled capitalism, but understood politically, anarchy has more often been seen as a threat to the social and economic order established under liberal-capitalist auspices. No sane disciple of Locke would agree with Proudhon that property is theft. Yet in truth anarchist theory need not be anticapitalist or antiliberal. (As much is affirmed by the very name chosen by libertarian anarchists to describe their doctrine: anarchocapitalism.) A distinct tradition of anarchist thought built on essentially Lockean principles stretches back across almost two centuries. At one end of this tradition we find William Godwin, the English philosopher and political reformer whose *Enquiry Concerning Political Justice* (1793) is a major landmark in the history of anarchist thought. Less well known to modern readers is a school of nineteenth-century American anarchists typified by Lysander Spooner, a Boston lawyer best remembered as a radical abolitionist. A look at the theories of Godwin and Spooner will serve as a prelude to our discussion of today's libertarian anarchists.

Our first task, however, will be to uncover the Lockean paradigm at the root of liberal and libertarian anarchism. This task can best be accomplished through a close analysis of several chapters of Locke's *Second Treatise*. Locke provides a model for an anarchist society in his original portrait of the state of nature, but finds the model plagued with difficulties that, in his view, necessitate the introduction of government. Liberal and libertarian anarchists, then, seek in effect to recreate Locke's state of nature. The viability of their project ultimately turns on the plausibility of Locke's model and on the possibility of overcoming the defects he found insurmountable.

Locke's State of Nature

Locke introduces the state of nature in Chapter 2 of the *Second Treatise*. It is immediately apparent that the state of nature is not a historical location, but rather an escape from history. It affords Locke a pristine social environment in which people are free of habitual allegiance to any historical politics. We might say that the state of nature functions as a political *tabula rasa*. When we first encounter man in the state of nature he is independent of his fellows, though not antisocial. Acknowledging the law of nature, which Locke equates with reason itself, he understands "that all being equal and independent, no one ought to harm another in his Life, Health, Liberty, or Possessions."[1] The law of nature teaches self-preservation as well, and also, obliges each man to preserve the rest of mankind so long as his own safety "comes not in competition."

It is in discussing the right of self-preservation that Locke first hints at discord. The right of self-preservation, he explains, gives rise to the "strange doctrine" by which in the state of nature every man is executor of the natural law. This "strange doctrine" (the adjective is Locke's) gives every man the right to punish those who transgress the law of nature *and to be judge of the transgression*. As each man is thus judge in his own case, Locke admits that want of a final authority to settle disputes may lead to what he disarmingly terms "inconveniences."[2]

Exactly what Locke means by "inconvenience" is not immediately apparent. One thing, however, is clear: Locke does not intend to convey that the state of nature, as described in Chapter 2, is identical with the state of war introduced in Chapter 3. Alluding to Hobbes, Locke complains that some political thinkers have indeed confounded the two situations. He, on the other hand, is careful to distinguish between them. The one he describes as a state of "Enmity, Malice, Violence, and Mutual Destruction," the other as a state of "Peace, Good Will, Mutual Assistance, and Preservation." Beyond this mere behavioral difference lies a moral distinction. "Want of a common Judge with Authority, puts all Men in a State of Nature: Force without Right, upon a Man's

Person, makes a State of War, both where there is, and where there is not, a common Judge."[3] Of no little consequence to his argument, Locke notes that the mere threat of force (without right) is equivalent to the actual use of force in bringing about the state of war.[4]

If for Locke nature may be inconvenient, war is always calamitous. Eventually people take refuge from both inconvenience and calamity in the safe haven of civil society. Government is established through adoption of the social compact. Certainly, a decision to escape the state of "Enmity, Malice, Violence, and Mutual Destruction," even at the cost of personal freedom, is understandable; but why is Locke so quick to abandon the state of "Peace, Good Will, Mutual Assistance, and Preservation"? Locke confronts this question in Chapter 9 of the *Second Treatise*. There he asks:

> If Man in the State of Nature be so free, as has been said; if he be absolute Lord of his own Person and Possessions, equal to the greatest, and subject to no Body, why will he part with his Freedom? Why will he give up this Empire, and subject himself to the Dominion and Controul of any other Power?

Locke's answer to this puzzle is that the state of nature affords no security of person or property! In a dramatic turnabout, he now writes that people in the state of nature are "constantly exposed to the Invasion of others" because the majority are "no strict Observers of Equity and Justice."[5]

We might well ask how it is that people come to violate the law of nature when its precepts were earlier said to be easily discerned by all rational creatures. To the contrary, Locke now claims that people may be ignorant of the natural law "for want of study of it," or, biased in their own behalf, they may simply exempt themselves from its requirements. Hence the law of nature will be, if not entirely unknown, then at least unsettled and unestablished. The lack of a common judge with final authority precludes the uniform interpretation of the law. Lack of a sovereign power to back the law means there can be no guarantee of its enforcement. No longer a state of peace, goodwill, and mutual assistance, the state of nature has become a world of fear and "continual dangers."[6] Suddenly there seems little distance between the inconvenience of nature and the calamity of war.

It is evident that Locke's discussion of the state of nature is less straightforward than it first appeared to be. Within the space of seven chapters the benign environment to which we are initially introduced has become intolerable. If there was little reason to leave the peaceful state of nature described in Chapter 2, there is every reason to flee the anxiety-inducing state of nature revealed in Chapter 9. Are we to conclude that Locke was being hypocritical, ridiculing Hobbes while covertly (or not so covertly) repeating the Hobbesian formula equating the states of nature and war?[7] It is difficult to believe Locke guilty of so clumsy a subterfuge. But then how are we to explain the paradox? I think a satisfactory answer may be produced if we understand Locke to have given us not one but two states of nature. It remains to be seen how the first is transformed into the second. To uncover that process we must examine Locke on property and the family, discussions that lie in the chapters separating the first and second states of nature.

Locke begins his chapter on property (Chapter 5) by citing both reason and revelation in evidence of an original equality of condition in the world. Reason instructs "that Men, being once born, have a right to their Preservation, and consequently to Meat and Drink, and such other things, as Nature affords for their Subsistence." Meanwhile, Scripture provides an account "of those grants God made of the World to *Adam,* and to *Noah,* and his Sons [from which] 'tis very clear, that God, as King *David* says, Psal. CXV, xvi, *has given the Earth to the Children of Men,* given it to Mankind in common.[8] Locke then defines his task in this chapter of the *Treatise* as tracing the origin of private property. With a slight shift in emphasis Locke's task might easily be described as an inquiry into the origins of inequality, making this chapter of the *Treatise* a Lockean version of Rousseau's second *Discourse.*

Despite his initial statements concerning the testimony of reason and scripture, Locke has no difficulty in finding a reasonable justification for private property. He first asserts that all men have a property in themselves (their physical bodies), and goes on to argue that the possession of things is made possible (and legitimate) by the "mixture" of self and object through labor.

> Though the Earth, and all inferior Creatures be common to all Men, yet every Man has a *Property* in his own *Person*. This no Body has any Right to but himself. The *Labour* of his Body, and the *Work* of his Hands, we may say, are properly his. Whatsoever then he removes out of the State that Nature hath provided, and left in, he hath mixed his *Labour* with, and joyned to it something that is his own, and thereby makes it his *Property*.

The assimilation of object to self renders property inviolable, or in Locke's terms, "excludes the common right of other Men."[9]

There are limits to accumulation, however. Locke concludes the passage just quoted with the following proviso: " . . .*Labour* being the unquestionable Property of the Labourer, no Man but he can have a right to what is once joyned to, *at least where there is enough, and as good left in common for others.*"[10] Thus there is a morally imposed limit to the amount any one man can appropriate from the common stock. Moreover, nature itself places a limit on accumulation, because "no Mans Labour could subdue, or appropriate all." Hence there was once a time when "it was impossible for any Man . . . to intrench upon the right of another, or acquire, to himself, a Property, to the Prejudice of his Neighbour." The extent of his property limited by the scope of his labors, even the most industrious man left behind "enough and as good" in common for others. In this context, what Locke calls the "conveniency of Life" helps generate a second moral limitation on private property: given the barrier to accumulation imposed by nature, Locke holds that no one should—and indeed no one could reasonably want to—claim more for himself than he actually could make use of. To illustrate this rule Locke explains that no one should gather more food than can be eaten before it spoils.[11] Thus far in Locke's account, owing to the general equality of condition that prevails despite the introduction of private ownership, the law of nature and human convenience coincide.

To this point Locke's discussion of property is ahistorical and might well be set in the (first) state of nature. It turns out, however, that the rise of inequality can be explained only by reference to a historical dynamic that the state of nature lacks.

Locke has recourse to what might be termed a natural history of property. He identifies conditions in the state of nature with "the first Ages of the World," when all the earth was a vast wilderness, and he points to the American wilderness of his own time as a likely example of what men confronted. All the world might yet be like America, he insists, were it not for a momentous innovation that transformed the concept of property.

> This I dare boldly affirm, That the same *Rule of Property* (viz.) that every Man should have as much as he could make use of, would hold still in the World, without straitning any body, since there is Land enough in the World to suffice double the Inhabitants had not the *Invention of Money,* and the tacit Agreement of Men to put a value on it, introduced (by Consent) larger Possessions, and a Right to them . . . .[12]

The agreement to place a value on pieces of metal that could not perish made it possible to accumulate property beyond anyone's need for immediate consumption. "And as different degrees of Industry were apt to give men Possessions in different Proportions, so this *Invention of Money* gave them the opportunity to enlarge them."[13] In the state of nature, or its historical equivalent, even the most industrious man could not far excel his indolent neighbor in amassing wealth; with the introduction of money, he could. Use no longer being a constraint on possession, the commons disappears and with it the general equality of condition guaranteed by equal access to the common stock.

Locke hardly considers this a great misfortune. While the invention of money dictates an artificial scarcity for some (because property is now inequitably distributed), it also provides a spur to industry and thus promotes the advance of civilization. Before the invention of money, according to Locke, people had little incentive to engage in strenuous labor; a benevolent nature provided an ample if somewhat primitive fare. Like the nomadic American Indians, all subsisted on acorns and clothed themselves with leaves and skins. For Locke, it is the incentive to labor provided by scarcity that moves one from savagery to civilization.

> There cannot be a clearer demonstration of any thing, than several Nations of the *Americans* are of this, who are rich in Land, and poor in all the Comforts of Life; whom Nature having furnished as liberally as any other people, with the materials of Plenty, *i.e.,* a fruitful Soil, apt to produce in abundance, what might serve for food, rayment and delight; yet for want of improving it by labour, have not one hundredth of the Conveniences we enjoy: And a King of a large and fruitful territory there feeds, lodges, and is clad worse than a day Labourer in England.[14]

So highly does Locke value the incentive to labor that he at one point describes as "godlike" the Prince who establishes laws for the encouragement of honest industry.[15]

It is in regard to the connection between labor and the progress of civilization that Locke introduces the labor theory of value. Labor not only creates a right to ownership, it improves on nature and thereby adds to the usefulness of natural objects; in this way labor creates value.[16] And it is because labor and the creation of value are tied up with property that Locke is able to get around the proviso enjoining men to leave "enough and as good" for the rest of mankind. Disingenuously, Locke argues that "he who appropriates land to himself by his labour, does not lessen but increase the common stock of mankind."[17] His argument rests on the claim that cultivation (or, more generally, industry) increases the bounty of nature many times over. Thus the usurpation of the commons is morally allowable because the improvements wrought by industry actually increase the stock of goods in the world. But Locke ignores the fact that these goods will not be equally accessible to all. It is by no means clear that even a general rise in the standard of living would meet the conditions set by the proviso; anticipating the posture of liberal political economists, Locke casually appears to assume that it would.

Here we do well to consider that if the first state of nature, or its historical equivalent, is devoid of industry, it is also a realm without discord. Where all have equal access to the common stock and are able to appropriate only what they have need of and can actually use, no one is deprived by what another takes for himself, and, more important, no one is apt to consider himself deprived. In this situation, to use Locke's phrase, right and convenience go together.[18] That is, people behave rightly because it is convenient (or reasonable from the standpoint of personal utility) for them to do so. Put another way, there are no thieves because there is no motive to theft. Nor in the bountiful, if primitive, state of nature do we expect to find acrimonious disputes over property rights. With "enough and as good" left over for all, who would bother to contest any individual's claim to some particular good? In short, conditions in the first state of nature promote adherence to natural law.

The introduction of inequality (through the invention of money) marks a significant alteration of this environment. Those deprived of nature's bounty and denied access to the improvements worked by the owners of property are given a powerful motive to become thieves. Thus it is only after the invention of money that people have reason to fear for the security of life and property. It is at this point that the state of nature is likely to evolve into a state of war, because right and convenience have been divorced. With the invention of money and the subsequent rise of inequality we have entered the *second* state of nature, a realm of thieves and their victims, who will gladly exchange freedom for security.[19]

Thus Locke's natural history of property takes us from the first into the second state of nature, where the need of government is clearly evident. Yet Locke's discussion of property is strangely silent about politics. This omission seems all the more curious in that we are led to believe that the philosophically useful "natural history" corresponds to a historically valid developmental sequence. Because it begins and ends in the politically timeless state of nature, however, Locke's history of property can tell us nothing about historical politics. Looking beyond the state-of-nature argument, which yields an ahistorical politics of consent (the social compact), we are unable to account for the origin of government. We must look elsewhere in the *Treatise* for Locke's views on this question.

Locke offers a historical perspective on original government in his discussion of the family. At the same time he addresses the problem of political allegiance and confronts a serious challenge to the politics of consent not previously encountered. To begin with, in discussing the family Locke broadens his account of human nature. When he earlier described man in the state of nature he emphasized human rationality. His portrait of human behavior suggested a population motivated by rational self-interest. People in the (first) state of nature look after themselves and their property and leave their peaceable neighbors to do the same. These people are not incapable of fellow feeling, but whatever sympathies they may have for one another are not likely to become politically significant. Rational beings are capable of collective action only through the mechanism of contract. There is no question of political allegiance in their society, merely the personal obligation to honor one's promises. In discussing the family, however, Locke makes reason subordinate to affection and discovers the root of political loyalty in the web of kinship ties and the binding cement of filial piety.

Locke describes the family as a natural association arising from the union of male and female and perpetuated by their instinctive parental concern for their offspring.[20] Parental authority is compatible with natural law and the rightful autonomy of every rational person owing to the child's immaturity. (Unlike the idiot or the madman, every child is potentially rational, but requires the guidance of a fully rational adult until coming of age.)[21] In the state of nature rationality bestows freedom, and parents have no claim to authority over their grown children. But in Chapter 8 ("The Beginning of Political Societies") Locke suggests that the family evolved into a political unit with the father as ruler.

> For the Father having, by the Law of Nature, the same Power
> with every Man else to punish, as he saw fit, any Offences
> against that Law, might thereby punish his transgressing Chil-
> dren even when they where Men, and out of their Pupilage; and
> they were very likely to submit to his punishment, and all joyn
> with him against the Offender, in their turns, giving him there-
> by power to Execute his Sentence against any transgression, and
> so in effect make him the Lawmaker, and Governour over all
> that remained in Conjunction with his Family. He was fittest to
> be trusted; Paternal affection secured their Property, and Interest
> under his Care, and the Custom of obeying him, in their Child-
> hood, made it easier to submit to him, rather than to any
> other.[22]

Locke supposes that in the first governments either the father's
authority was transferred to the eldest son or else the father's role
was assumed by a general in time of war. So it was that "the first
Beginners of Common-Wealths generally put the Rule into one
Man's hand, without any other express Limitation or Restraint,
but what the Nature of the thing, and the End of Government
required."[23] Benevolent father-rulers ensured "the publick Good
and Safety." Here Locke presents a road to civil society strikingly different from the path leading out of the state of nature.
He makes an attempt at reconciling the two by defining all political authority as a trust pledging rulers to ends desired by those
they govern.[24] But this stipulation serves to free sons of absolute
obedience to their father-rulers only if men are willing to examine their loyalties by rational standards. Postulating criteria by
which an act of government or the government itself may be
declared illegitimate does not guarantee that the criteria will be
employed; a *right* of revolution cannot provide a *motive* to revolution capable of dissolving the emotional ties or habits of allegiance binding men to their traditional rulers. Locke offers us no
reason to believe that sentimental attachments and habitual allegiance will falter in the event beloved father-rulers become
thieves.*

*On this point Gordon J. Schochet goes astray. He argues that Locke's

Locke has established the father-ruler as a charismatic figure whose authority rests on the spontaneous loyalty of his subjects—in Lockean terms, on trust—rather than on their consent. He immediately locates this original monarchy in a lost Golden Age, a time before ambition and luxury had corrupted the state and "taught Princes to have distinct and separate Interests from their People."[25] We see that Locke's historical account of original government centered on the family has begun to run parallel to his earlier history of property. Consider the following description of the Golden Age:

> The equality of a simple poor way of liveing confining their desires within the narrow bounds of each mans smal propertie made few controversies and so no need of many laws to decide them: And there wanted not Justice where there were but few Trespasses, and few Offenders. . . . And therefore their first care and thought cannot but be supposed to be, how to secure themselves against foreign Force. 'Twas natural for them to put themselves under a *Frame of Government,* which might best serve to that end; and chuse the wisest and bravest Man to conduct them in their Wars, and lead them out against their Enemies, and in this chiefly to be their *Ruler.*[26]

As in the first ages of the world, when all things were held in common and there was little reason to fear thieves, people who lived during the Golden Age, before the introduction of luxury, had little reason to fear their rulers. Clearly, the father-ruler or his military equivalent had precious little to do in time of peace, even though Locke had earlier described him as a lawmaker.[27]

If we combine Locke's two histories, we see that the father-ruler is likely to emerge as a lawmaker and true executive only

---

discussion of the evolution of monarchy from parental authority is designed to show "that the familial origins of government were of no value in understanding the nature of man's subsequent political communities" ("The Family and the Origins of the State in Locke's Political Philosophy," in *John Locke: Problems and Perspectives,* ed. J. W. Yolton [Cambridge: Cambridge University Press, 1969], p. 98). In fact, Locke's account of the transformation of paternal authority reveals most strikingly the threat posed to a politics of consent by a charismatic leader (metaphorically, the father).

after the invention of money (and the subsequent rise of inequality) has created the need for one. But it is precisely at this
historical juncture that the benign father-ruler is most apt to
become a tyrant-thief, for it is the arrival of a money economy
that facilitates an age of corrupting luxury. The only way to
guard against the prince turned thief is to replace the politics of
trust with the politics of consent, exchanging the father-ruler for
a "phantom executive" with no will of his own. Unlike the
father, the executive established by the politics of consent "is to
be consider'd as the Image, Phantom, or Representative of the
Commonwealth, acted by the will of the Society, declared in its
Laws; and thus he has no Will, no Power, but that of the Law."[28]

Unfortunately, Locke has the logic of consent unfold in the
first state of nature, where, because right and convenience go
together, all people are inclined to obey natural law as a matter of
course. Where the politics of consent is truly needed, in the
second state of nature, Locke tells us that rationality is in short
supply and the precepts of natural law are largely ignored. It
appears that Locke has painted himself into a corner. Paradoxically, the minimal state he advocates is feasible only where any
government is superfluous.

It can be argued that in setting up the second state of nature
Locke justified the minimal state but left it inaccessible. The
anarchists who follow in Locke's footsteps face an analogous
problem. The possibility of anarchism suggested by the first
(premonetary) state of nature is seemingly removed by entry into
the second (postmonetary) state of nature. Working within the
Lockean framework, the anarchist is burdened to find a path that
will lead back to the idyllic world where right and convenience
go together. Consequently, the problem central to anarchist theory is not the state but inequality.

William Godwin and the Dissolution of Government

One of the first political thinkers who deserves to be called a
libertarian anarchist is William Godwin (1756–1836). Philoso-

pher, novelist, and political reformer, Godwin was a leading figure among the bourgeois radicals who preached the rights of man to king and country in late-eighteenth-century Britain.[29] His *Enquiry Concerning Political Justice,* first published in 1793, ranks as a major work in the literature of anarchism.[30] There Godwin in his own way confronts the Lockean dilemma.

Godwin begins *Political Justice* by acknowledging the paradox Locke would rather ignore: that the state, which was established to hang thieves and ensure justice, is in a position to become the biggest thief of all. "Government," he writes, "was intended to suppress injustice, but offers new occasions and temptations for the commission of it." Nor does Godwin hesitate when it comes to assigning the root cause of injustice. What Locke admits only by implication Godwin asserts outright: it is inequality of condition that makes thieves. And here, too, government only serves to make matters worse: "By perpetuating and aggravating the inequality of property, it fosters many injurious passions, and excites men to the practice of robbery and fraud."[31] One need not read past the Statement of Principles at the front of the book to realize that Godwin considers the social contract a bad bargain. Clearly, the ills occasioned by government outweigh any good to be found in the state.

If we use the *Second Treatise* as a frame of reference, *Political Justice* may be located in the second state of nature. Godwin takes as given a social environment where inequality has divorced right from convenience. Consequently, the requirements of justice and morality are slighted in the pursuit of self-interest. In Godwin's analysis,

> the spirit of oppression, the spirit of servility, and the spirit of fraud . . . are the immediate growth of the established administration of property. They are alike hostile to intellectual and moral improvement. The other vices of envy, malice and revenge are their inseparable companions.

Godwin immediately contrasts this dismal reality with an optimistic vision of what might be, were there equality of condition.

> In a state of society where men lived in the midst of plenty, and where all shared alike the bounties of nature, these sentiments would inevitably expire. The narrow principle of selfishness would vanish. No man being obliged to guard his little store, or provide, with anxiety and pain, for his restless wants, each would lose his individual existence, in the thought of the general good. No man would be an enemy to his neighbor, for there would be no subject of contention. . . . [32]

To revert again to the language of the *Second Treatise,* equality would reunite right and convenience, establishing peace by removing the occasion for conflict. Politically, people would move backward from the second state of nature to the first (though surely Godwin would label this movement progress).

Despite his views on equality, Godwin is no leveler. He dismisses a resort to coercion as being neither just nor wise and looks upon any political solution as impractical. Moreover, he supports the right to unlimited accumulation so long as no person invades the rightfully acquired property of others.[33] How, then, is equality of condition to be introduced? Godwin's answer is that people are to be rationally persuaded of the benefits inherent in a system of general equality, and they must voluntarily create a new society that reflects their shared conviction. "Persuasion, and not force," he writes, "is the legitimate instrument for influencing the human mind; and I shall never be justifiable in having recourse to the latter, while there is any rational hope of succeeding by the former."[34]

Ultimately it is not a Lockean concept of property that Godwin defends but "the sacred and indefeasible right of private judgment." In opposing a coercive redistributive solution to the problem of inequality, Godwin is defending the individual's moral autonomy.

> The first idea of property . . . is a reduction from the right of private judgment; the first object of government is the preservation of this right. Without permitting every man, to a considerable degree, the exercise of his own discretion, there can be no independence, no improvement, no virtue and no happiness.[35]

It is now apparent that for Godwin equality is a necessary but not a sufficient cause of social harmony. People must first be persuaded to choose equality; a revolution in popular morals must precede the dissolution of government.

Godwin is confident that he can persuade others to accept his radical ideas. To his mind it is not merely a matter of persuasion, but a question of truth and human rationality. Godwin subscribes to a doctrine of necessity that holds voluntary actions to be "in all instances conformable to the deductions of . . . understanding." In other words, rational comprehension of truth provides a sufficient and compelling motive to right action. Moreover, the nature of the human mind is such that "sound reasoning and truth, when adequately communicated, must always be victorious over error."[36]

> There is, in reality, little room for skepticism respecting the omnipotence of truth. Truth is the pebble in the lake; and, however slowly, in the present case, the circles succeed each other, they will infallibly go on, till they overspread the surface. No order of mankind will forever remain ignorant of the principles of justice, equality and public good. No sooner will they understand them than they will perceive the coincidence of virtue and public good with private interest: Nor will any erroneous establishment be able effectually to support itself against general opinion. In this contest sophistry will vanish, and mischievous institutions sink quietly into neglect. Truth will bring down all her forces, mankind will be her army, and oppression, injustice, monarchy and vice, will tumble in a common ruin.[37]

Placing himself in the vanguard of the army of truth, Godwin teaches that justice requires each individual to act for the common welfare. Pursuing the nature of that requirement, he asks, "How much am I bound to do for the general weal, that is, for the benefit of the individuals of whom the whole is composed?" The Rousseauistic answer to this question is "Everything in my power." Like Rousseau, who taught that selfish desires must be subordinated to the larger moral authority of the general will, Godwin insists that we ought to value the wellbeing of the community above our own personal welfare. In the extreme, we should be willing to sacrifice our very lives for the greater good. "If the extraordinary case should occur in which I can promote the general good by my death more than by my life, justice requires that I should be content to die." Godwin does not expect frequent need of such heroics, however. Under ordinary circumstances justice requires not that we die but that we live for the community. We are to use whatever talents and abilities we possess to advance the well-being of others. Persons of wealth and property are to employ their riches to benefit the public. Talents and wealth, Godwin explains, ought to be regarded as advantages held in trust in behalf of mankind.[38]

Though Godwin's conception of moral responsibility turns private individuals into public actors and vitiates the Lockean concept of private property (for Godwin, every shilling of personal wealth is "appropriated by the laws of morality"), he resists the temptation to politicize morality by giving the principles of justice the force of law. "Truth and virtue are competent to fight their own battles," he explains. "They do not need to be nursed and patronized by the hand of power."[39] And yet we may ask, do not the principles of justice require some external sanction? After all, even the good are sometimes weak, and not all are good. Again sounding much like Rousseau, Godwin answers this objection by invoking the power of public opinion. The moral force of the community alone will superintend the requirements of justice. Godwin suggests that under "the empire of reason," offenders against justice are likely to amend their conduct once they are made to understand the error of their ways. Any offender who proved recalcitrant would certainly "feel so uneasy, under the unequivocal disapprobation, and observant eye, of public judgment, as willingly to remove to a society more congenial to his errors."[40]

Godwin is not advocating a meaningless conformity achieved through peer pressure; on the contrary, we are expected to embrace his system knowingly, convinced of its truth. Reason teaches all who will listen that right and convenience go together; or, in Godwin's words, that justice, morality, and the public good are "coincident with each man's private advantage." Having been brought to a correct understanding of morality, we will abandon the inequality that creates a need of government. Where the principles of justice are universally acknowledged, "no man will have the least desire for purposes of ostentation or luxury, to possess more than his neighbours."[41] In short, Godwin argues that rational beings will not choose to live under conditions analogous to Locke's second state of nature; rather, they will voluntarily recreate the social and economic conditions of the first. This will not be an equality "introduced by force, or maintained by the laws and regulations of a positive institution," or "the result of accident, of the authority of a chief magistrate, or the over-earnest persuasion of a few enlightened thinkers," but a condition produced "by the serious and deliberate conviction of the public at large."[42]

Unlike Locke, who linked inequality to economic development and technological progress, Godwin does not envision the state of equality as "a state of Stoical simplicity." By his calculations, "the labour of half an hour *per diem* on the part of every individual in the community would probably be sufficient to procure for all the necessaries of life," and Godwin has little doubt that most people would spend the remainder of their day in the production of those things that "though not to be classed among the necessaries of life, are highly conducive to our well being."[43] Godwin is not asking us to give up the advantages of civilization. He is, however, rejecting the economic and social consequences of liberal capitalism. In effect, Godwin's anarchism, built on essentially Lockean assumptions, is an attempt to save liberalism from itself.

Lysander Spooner and "Individualist Anarchism" in Nineteenth-Century America

Anarchist doctrines have never flourished in America. We might well have expected all Americans to be anarchists under the skin, given the suspicion of the state that haunts our political tradition. Yet anarchism has rarely been preached and even more rarely has met a sympathetic reception. To the popular imagination, anarchy has always seemed somehow foreign, a bit of corruption imported from the old world and completely out of place in the new. But the popular imagination is not historically accurate; American anarchists did not always speak with a foreign accent, nor were their ideas necessarily alien to the essentially Lockean American world view. Just as the Englishman William Godwin fashioned a case for anarchism from the philosophic materials bequeathed by Locke, Lysander Spooner and other nineteenth-century American radicals also turned Lockean arguments to anarchist conclusions. A historian sympathetic to their ideas has labeled Spooner and his fellow dissenters from mainstream American liberalism "individualist anarchists."[44] The label fits, for their grand object, like Godwin's, was to secure the independence and moral autonomy of the individual.

Typical of the individualist anarchist position are the writings of Lysander Spooner (1808–1887).* Lawyer and radical abolitionist, Spooner was a prolific pamphleteer and eager polemicist.[45] Whether his subject was slavery, poverty, or natural law, he invariably traced the ills of this world to the machinations of governments. Although he never declared himself an anarchist, it is clear he had little use for the state and would have preferred that civil society be organized as a voluntary association.†

The view of human society found in Spooner's *Natural Law; or the Science of Justice* might easily have been lifted from the *Second*

---

*My choice of Spooner is owed partly to convenience; the body of his work has been reprinted in recent years and is more generally accessible than that of other representative thinkers. Beyond mere convenience, Spooner is the one figure among the "individualist anarchists" singled out by the modern anarchocapitalist Murray Rothbard in *For a New Liberty: The Libertarian Manifesto*, rev. ed. (New York: Collier Books, 1978). It was Rothbard's special fondness for Spooner that first brought him to my attention.

†Of the so-called individualist anarchists discussed in James J. Martin's *Men against the State: The Expositors of Individualist Anarchism in America* (De Kalb, Ill.: Adrian Allen, 1953), only Benjamin Tucker actually employed the anarchist label, which he borrowed from Proudhon. Still, I believe Martin correctly describes Spooner's thought as anarchistic.

Treatise. Spooner argues that rational self-interest instructs all people in the precepts of natural law by teaching them to distinguish one individual's property from another's.[46] Consequently, "almost all men have the same perceptions of what constitutes justice, or of what justice requires, when they understand alike the facts from which their inferences are drawn."[47] As it turns out, what justice requires is for each individual to respect the inviolability of person and property. So long as all seek to live justly and refrain from doing injustice, peace reigns. Where the requirements of justice are foresaken, "men are at war. And they must necessarily remain at war until justice is reestablished."[48] As with Locke, civil society emerges as an alternative to war and as a means of escaping the "inconveniences" of nature. Spooner writes that although all people have a natural right

> to repel injustice, and to compel justice, for themselves, and for all who may be wronged, yet to avoid the errors that are liable to result from haste and passion, and that everybody, who desires it, may rest secure in the assurance of protection, without a resort to force, it is evidently desireable that men should associate, so far as they freely and voluntarily can do so, for the maintenance of justice among themselves, and for mutual protection against wrong-doers.[49]

Spooner likens this voluntary association for the maintenance of justice to the purchase of insurance against fire or commercial loss. Far from involving any political motives or suggesting any question of allegiance, it is wholly a matter of contract.

Spooner's radical contractarianism led him to deny that any obedience was due the United States government as it then existed. In the first of his *No Treason* pamphlets (1867) he calls people dunces for "uniting to sustain any government, or any laws, *except those in which* they are all agreed." And consent must be unanimous, requiring "the separate, individual consent of every man who is required to contribute, either by taxation or personal service, to the support of government."[50] In subsequent issues of the *No Treason* series Spooner disputes the legal authority of the

United States Constitution, contending that as a contractual document it falsely presumes the express consent of the American people.[51] In point of fact, Spooner argues, the Constitution was a contract among its framers and binding only on the small minority that ratified it; the Founding Fathers had no right to act for anyone other than themselves, and their commitments bound no other persons, let alone future generations.[52]

Clearly, a government that claims authority on the basis of an invalid social contract is itself illegitimate. In the *No Treason* pamphlets Spooner describes the government of the United States as a Lockean tyrant-thief.

> It is true that the *theory* of our Constitution is . . . that our government is a mutual insurance company, voluntarily entered into by the people with each other; that each man makes a free and purely voluntary contract with all others who are parties to the Constitution, to pay so much money for so much protection, the same as he does with any other insurance company; and that he is just as free not to be protected, and not to pay tax, as he is to pay a tax, and be protected. But this theory of our government is wholly different from the practical fact. The fact is that the government, like a highwayman, says to a man: 'Your money, or your life.' And many, if not most, taxes are paid under compulsion of that threat.[53]

At least the highwayman does not insult his victim, Spooner exclaims. The acknowledged thief does not claim that he acts for the benefit of those he robs.*

---

*Nothing that Spooner said of the American government was intended to apply with less force to any other historical government.

> All the great governments of the world—those now existing, as well as those that have passed away—have been of this character. They have been mere bands of robbers, who have associated for purposes of plunder, conquest, and the enslavement of their fellow men. And their laws, as they have called them, have been only such agreements as they have found it necessary to enter into, in order to maintain their organizations, and act together in plundering and enslaving others, and in securing to each his agreed share of the spoils. [*Natural Law,* in *The Collected Works of Lysander Spooner,* ed. Charles Shively, 6 vols. (Weston, Mass.: M & S Press, 1971), 1:18 (pagination follows the original)]

People may well be dunces for giving allegiance to a tyrant-thief, yet as Spooner himself notes, dunces are never in short supply. Acknowledging the reality of political allegiance, he admits that it "is not improbable that many or most of the worst governments—although established by force, and by a few, in the first place—come, in time, to be supported by a majority."[54] To Spooner this support indicates only the ignorance and servility of which people are capable. Like Godwin before him, Spooner would combat ignorance with enlightenment. He tells his fellow Americans that they have been duped into thinking themselves free because some among them (white male propertyholders) can vote. "A man is none the less a slave," he argues, "because he is allowed to choose a new master once in a term of years."[55]

As an anarchist among democrats, for whom the voice of the people speaks at the ballot box, Spooner makes the act of voting a primary target of his polemical assault. He complains that where the voter has no option to reject government altogether, the casting of one's ballot is no true expression of consent to be governed. Voting under these circumstances is more correctly understood as an act of self-defense. Men vote, Spooner writes, in the hope of electing a regime that will enslave others but not themselves. As for the secret ballot, the supposed guarantee of free elections and the voters' independence, Spooner has only condemnation. Secrecy makes it impossible to know the voter's intention and erases his signature from the social contract. Elected officials are left accountable to no one, as it is impossible to identify the voters who cast their ballots for the victors.[56] Thus government is denied even the possibility of legitimacy and tyrant-thieves are enabled to hide behind a vague electoral mandate.

The question earlier asked of Locke and Godwin has still to be asked of Spooner: Why is it that some men become thieves and aspire to be tyrant-thieves? Spooner provides a familiar answer in his pamphlet *Poverty: Its Illegal Causes and Legal Cure* (1846). There he explains that crime is a result of poverty and the fear of poverty, which drives people to desperate measures. Poverty, in turn, is a sign of maldistributed wealth and a pernicious inequality that denies the majority enjoyment of the fruits of their own labor.

> The wheel of fortune, in the present state of things, is of such enormous diameter; those on its top are on so showy a height; and those underneath it are in such a pit of debt, oppression, and despair; and its revolutions are so rapid, unsteady and convulsive, that it is no subject of wonder that those on its sides should feel compelled, by the necessity of self-preservation, to jostle and cheat each other out of their footing, in order to secure one for themselves.

To correct this situation Spooner proposes reforms under which

> fortune could hardly be represented by a wheel; for it would present no such height, no such depth, no such irregularity of motion as now. It should rather be represented by an extended surface, varied somewhat by inequalities, but still exhibiting a general level, affording a safe position for all, and creating no necessity, for either force or fraud, on the part of any one, to enable him to secure his standing.[57]

To employ once again the language of the *Second Treatise,* right and convenience are to be reunited. Like Godwin, Spooner proposes to lead us from Locke's second state of nature to the more equitable conditions of the first.

The reforms Spooner suggests all aim toward loosening the existing restrictions on credit, which prevent "the natural and more equal diffusion of credit among all those poor men, who are in want of capital upon which to bestow their labor, and who, for want of such capital, are compelled to sell their labor to others for a price much below the amount of its actual product."[58] Rejecting the system of wage labor as inherently corrupt, Spooner argues that every man ought to be his own employer, and he envisions a world of yeoman farmers and independent entrepreneurs made possible by the easy availability of credit. He believes that were each man to appropriate the fruits of his own labor, the distribution of wealth would be nearly equal and re-cognizably just.[59]

No more than Godwin does Spooner share Locke's foreboding that a rough equality of condition will doom humankind to savagery. "The mind of man is fertile of invention almost beyond conception," he boasts.

> All it needs is stimulus and opportunity to develop itself. And that condition is neither of poverty, nor riches; but of moderate competency—such as will neither enervate him by luxury, nor disable him by destitution; but which will at once give him an opportunity to labor, (both mentally and physically) and stimulate him by offering him all the fruits of his labors.[60]

Moreover, a rough equality of condition will help promote the sense of community destroyed by that gross inequality which creates a sense of caste.[61] At the same time, the elimination of poverty and great wealth will do away with the vices, such as gambling, intemperance, and lewdness, which are common among rich and poor alike but shunned by those of "moderate competence."[62] Finally, in a society of equals ambition will not lead individuals to seek political advantage over their neighbors. Spooner predicts that "preeminent minds, that are now employed and exhausted in the projection and execution of great plans of rapacity and power, in fierce struggles for the elevation of the few, and the corresponding prostration of the many, would be driven, by a sort of moral necessity, to seek more peaceful employments."[63]

The parallels that can be seen in the works of Spooner and Godwin strongly suggest that they share a common ideological universe. Their fundamental assumptions are essentially Lockean, to the extent that we may use the logic of the *Second Treatise* as a guide through their arguments. In short, these anarchist thinkers are truly Lockean liberals, though liberals with a difference. While accepting the primacy of individual liberty, which is the distinctive mark of liberalism, they reject the inequality of condition that Locke found inevitable. Mainstream liberal theorists and political economists since Locke have tended to place liberty and equality in opposition, defending inequality as a necessary by-product of freedom. In opposition to this tide of liberal opinion, Spooner and Godwin insist that inequality corrupts freedom. Their anarchism is directed as much against inequality as against tyranny.

A certain naiveté pervades the arguments of both Spooner and Godwin. Each in his own way is given to millennial fantasies and utopian visions. But theirs is also a political naiveté characteristic of liberalism generally. The polity envisioned by Locke demands that we be apolitical. As we have seen, one of Locke's problems in the *Second Treatise* was to insulate rational, egoistic individuals from the charismatic appeal of father-rulers and tyrant-thieves. Later liberal theorists take for granted Locke's solution to this problem, often failing to remember that the problem exists at all, let alone that Locke's solution is at best ambivalent.* Neither Spooner nor Godwin shows much awareness of human motives outside the framework of Locke's state-of-nature argument. Within that framework, the rough condition of equality they both prescribe will eliminate the problem of theft among rational beings; but the unacknowledged problem of politics remains.

The irony here is that both Spooner and Godwin are critics of atomistic liberalism in search of community. To them, it is inequality that provokes the war of all against all. In consequence, they see a rough equality of condition as a guarantee of social harmony and the prerequisite to a true human community. Yet theirs, no less than Locke's, is conceived as a community of interests among self-regarding individuals. It is a "community" founded on convenience and nurtured by instrumental rationality. In short, it is the emotionally antiseptic "community" of Locke's first state of nature. However appealing to the liberal turned anarchist, this vision of community is unreal. Moreover,

---

*One need only look at the literature of classical political economy or contemporary economics to confirm this observation. Many of Locke's heirs appear to accept *Homo economicus,* that true denizen of the state of nature, as the end product of human evolution. Cf. Lester C. Thurow, *Dangerous Currents: The State of Economics* (New York: Random House, 1983).

it is very vulnerable. As Locke seemed aware, social bonds constructed of rational self-interest are fragile and easily overwhelmed by political passions.

It is possible to view Spooner and Godwin as critics of an emerging capitalist system; that is, of the dog-eat-dog social reality shaped by liberal capitalism in the nineteenth century. Their anarchism has an almost romantic flavor as they look forward to social harmony among self-regarding individualists. In fact, they have romanticized the liberal-capitalist ideal recognizable as Locke's first state of nature. People who inhabit the first state of nature are morally superior to those in the second, because they have not yet been corrupted by greed or ambition; their rough equality of condition is their badge of innocence. What Spooner and Godwin forget is that for Locke, this is a *lost* innocence. For better or worse, we live after the fall. For the liberal who remains wedded to the Lockean faith there can be no redemption. Our lot is to cope as best we can in the second state of nature.

5

The State of Nature Revisited: Libertarian Anarchocapitalism

Whatever services the government actually performs could be supplied far more efficiently and far more morally by private and cooperative enterprise.

—MURRAY ROTHBARD, *For a New Liberty*

MODERN anarchocapitalists such as Murray Rothbard and David Friedman are thoroughly at home in Locke's second state of nature. While sympathetic to Spooner's individualist anarchism, they fail to notice or conveniently overlook its egalitarian implications.[1] For them, equality is the battle cry of those who would oppress the individual in the name of the collectivity. They, on the contrary, accept inequality as the price of freedom. Moreover, unlike Spooner or Godwin, they harbor no reservations about the social consequences of capitalism. Anarchocapitalists are anarchists *because* they are capitalists.

Anarchocapitalism offers principled opposition to the state. As Rothbard explains, the libertarian creed

rests upon one central axiom: that no man or group of men may aggress against the person or property of anyone else.* . . . While opposing any and all private aggression against the rights of person and property, the libertarian sees that throughout history and into the present day, there has been one central, dominant, and overriding aggressor upon all of these rights: the State.[2]

*Rothbard considers true libertarianism synonymous with anarchocapitalism.

Following the definitions proposed by sociologists Max Weber and Franz Oppenheim, Rothbard conceives of the state as an instrument of coercion and condemns all forms of government to the role of aggressor. Not even the night-watchman state of classical liberalism is to be trusted, much less tolerated.[3] From Rothbard's perspective, a state is a state is a state; there are no differences in kind, merely differences in the degree of coercion.

> For centuries, the State (or more strictly, individuals acting in their roles as "members of the government") has cloaked its criminal activity in high-sounding rhetoric. For centuries the State has committed mass murder and called it "war" . . . For centuries the State has enslaved people into its armed battalions and called it "conscription" in "national service." For centuries the State has robbed people at bayonet point and called it "taxation." . . . If you wish to know how libertarians regard the State and any of its acts, simply think of the State as a criminal band, and all of the libertarian attitudes will logically fall into place.[4]

Rothbard's ringing denunciation of the State partakes more of political oratory than political analysis. (Indeed, it reads like the transcript of a stump speech.) Nevertheless, his claims merit serious consideration. Historically, states (if not the State) have waged wars, conscripted their citizens, and imposed heavy taxes all to the misfortune of their peoples. Of course, it is something else altogether to insist that the State (meaning every possible state) is inherently evil. That claim rests not on the historical record but on the theoretical criteria Rothbard employs. Given those criteria, no state ever could pass muster.

If Rothbard is highly sensitive to the historical state's invasion of individual rights, he is also curiously insensitive to the state's historical relationship with the market. He completely overlooks the role of the state in building and maintaining a capitalist economy in the West. Privileged to live in the twentieth century, long after the battles to establish capitalism have been fought and won, Rothbard sees the state solely as a burden on the market and a vehicle for imposing the still greater burden of socialism. He manifests a kind of historical nearsightedness that allows him to collapse many centuries of human experience into one long night of tyranny that ended only with the invention of the free market and its "spontaneous" triumph over the past.[5] It is pointless to argue, as Rothbard seems ready to do, that capitalism would have succeeded without the bourgeois state; the fact is that all capitalist nations have relied on the machinery of government to create and preserve the political and legal environments required by their economic system.[6]

On this point Rothbard seems to be unable to distinguish between economic theory and political reality. He is convinced that the "natural laws" of economics can do without the support of positive law. Since this proposition is logically consistent with his assumptions about the individual and society, he concludes that it must be true (indeed, it must always have been true) in fact. He is willing to concede some degree of collusion between capitalists and politicians only where corrupt businessmen have sought to gain an advantage for themselves by having the state impose legal barriers to competition.[7]* His constant focus is on

---

*In denouncing the corporate state, Rothbard cites with approval the works of Marxist historians Gabriel Kolko and James Weinstein, who have documented the role of business in the development of government regulation of the economy. When *Reason* magazine, a libertarian publication out of Los Angeles, put together a registry of scholars involved with libertarian issues, it asked Kolko if he would allow inclusion of his name. Kolko responded:

> Under no circumstances should I be listed in your Registry, or thought in any manner a supporter of your exotic political position. If anything proves my thesis that American conservative ideology is more a question of intelligence than politics, it has been the persistent use of my works to buttress your position. . . . As I made clear often and candidly to many so-called libertarians, I have been a socialist and against capitalism all of my life, my works are attacks on that system, and I have no common area of sympathy with the quaint irrelevancy called "free market" economics. There never has been such a system in historical reality, and if it ever comes into being you can count on me to favor its abolition. [*Reason* 5 (January 1974)]

Aside from its polemical intent, Kolko's response points toward the distinguishing feature of Rothbard's perspective on the corporate state. To Rothbard, the collusion between the state and business is the fault not of capitalism but of particular capitalists. The system is pure; only the individual is corrupt. Rothbard misses the point of the Marxist analysis, which discovers the origins of the corporate state in the dynamic of capitalism itself.

state intervention—particular state actions that disrupt the market—while the political guarantees that surround the market go unnoticed.

Such historical nearsightedness does not seem surprising, given Rothbard's predilection for abstraction (though, ironically, he has criticized others for being unhistorical).[8] Like Godwin and Spooner before him, Rothbard weaves a political theory that carries us back to Locke's ahistorical state of nature. Indeed, Rothbard turns to John Locke to justify the right of private property, at the same time borrowing the psychological assumptions that permit the Lockean politics of consent.[9] He ignores, however, the transformation of nature that occurs after the invention of money in Locke's account. As an anarchocapitalist he assumes that, at least for most persons, behavior appropriate to the first state of nature will continue in the second, despite Locke's assertion to the contrary.

It is this assumption that allows Rothbard to propose a market alternative to the state. Anarchocapitalism would turn over the police functions of the classical liberal state to private entrepreneurs whose services could be purchased—or refused—like any other economic good. Behaviorally, anarchocapitalism demands instrumental rationality and "economic" motives (Locke's politics of consent); it cannot tolerate "political" motives that unite persons in pursuit of ends the market cannot provide (Locke's politics of trust). Unfortunately for anarchocapitalism, it is impossible to contain the latter or completely to insulate the former from the threat of politics. Curiously, the architects of anarchocapitalism do not seem to be even vaguely aware of how vulnerable their system would be.

The anarchocapitalists apparently expect political motives simply to disappear with the demise of the state. Reflecting on the heated public controversies occasioned by such government policies as integration of the public schools and fluoridation of municipal water supplies, Rothbard observes:

> It should be clear that no such fierce arguments occur where each group of consumers can purchase the goods or services they

demand. There are no battles between consumers, for example, over what kind of newspaper should be printed, churches established, books printed, records marketed, automobiles manufactured.[10]

Evidently Rothbard believes that the practice of toleration is merely an economic artifact.

While it is tempting to believe that such naiveté is deliberate, there is no evidence to suggest that Rothbard does not honestly consider the profession of religious faith to be on a level with the choice of a new car. Here Rothbard is a true (if unwitting) disciple of Locke, for whom churches were properly mere voluntary societies, not the temporal armies of the Lord, rightly concerned only with the salvation of souls and not with "civil interests"— "life, liberty, health, and indolency of body; and the possession of outward things, such as money, lands, houses, furniture, and the like."[11] Locke's plea for toleration was designed to eliminate the political ills inflicted by religious fanaticism. But Locke's hopeful plea is Rothbard's casual assumption: that people will be sublimely indifferent to what their neighbors do and profess as long as their own property rights are respected.

In secular terms, Rothbard's anarchocapitalism is premised on the irrelevance of ideology. The privatization of belief made explicit in Locke's doctrine of toleration is reaffirmed implicitly by Rothbard's antipolitical doctrine. Echoing the Lockean theme, Rothbard focuses his attention on "civil interests," which belong to the outward world of works. What people believe is their own affair; what they do can affect others, and so a rule of right conduct is required. Anarchocapitalism maintains the liberal distinction between self-regarding acts, which, like matters of belief, are essentially private, and social acts, which are constrained by the right of property. Locke recognized that the wall between faith and works must not be breached, else belief may prompt an invasion of civil interests in the name of a higher good. For Locke, a state-enforced doctrine of toleration is the means of neutralizing what I have chosen to call "political" motives. Separated from the demands of faith, the world of works becomes the habitat of economic man.[12] Rothbard's anarchocapitalism requires the same protection from secular faiths that challenge the inviolability of private property. But the anarchocapitalists have deprived themselves of Locke's political solution.

What remains is reliance on the market itself to reinforce economic motives. Such a stance, of course, presumes the existence of an established market society. (To the extent that anarchocapitalists are able to take economic behavior for granted, they owe an unacknowledged debt to the liberal state, which did much to help mold that behavior.) A population socially adapted to the ways of the market is essential to the success of anarchocapitalism. Citizens and subjects are to be transformed into consumers for whom ultimate ends are essentially private and the means to those ends a matter of economic calculation.[13] The competition of buyers and sellers in the marketplace, an individualized competition of each against all, supplants the clash of organized interests in the political arena. Since, by definition, market transactions are perfectly voluntary, one cannot be coerced into accepting and paying for goods or services one does not want. The Lockean tyrant-thief is vanquished and we are suddenly back in the harmonious (first) state of nature. Or rather, because inequality prevails, we find ourselves in a hybrid state of nature that combines the material conditions of the second with the social environment of the first.

Anarchocapitalists spend a great deal of time extolling the superiority of their system and defending its practicality. That they believe their system is morally superior to statism should already be clear. The state employs coercion (necessarily); anarchocapitalism guarantees the (formal) freedom of market relations. But anarchocapitalism also lays claim to superior efficiency. Rothbard states the case thus:

> On the free market . . . the consumer is king, and any business firm that wants to make profits and avoid losses tries its best to serve the consumer as efficiently and at as low cost as possible. In a government operation, in contrast, everything changes. *Inherent in all government operation is a grave and fatal split between service and payment,* between the providing of a service and the payment for receiving it. The government bureau does not get

its income, as does the private firm, from serving the consumer well or from consumer purchases of its products exceeding the costs of operation. No, the government bureau acquires its income from mulcting the long-suffering taxpayer. Its operations therefore become inefficient, and costs zoom, since government bureaus need not worry about losses or bankruptcy; they can make up their losses by additional extractions from the public till. Furthermore, the consumer, instead of being courted and wooed for his favor, becomes a mere annoyance to the government, someone who is "wasting" the *government's* scarce resources. In government operations, the consumer is treated like an unwelcome intruder, an interference in the quiet enjoyment by the bureaucrat of his steady income.[14]

In short, once there is a market in "government" services, the citizen turned consumer can expect a better product and greater courtesy.

For those to whom market efficiency is best represented by the uniform mediocrity of fast-food restaurants and the artificial cheerfulness of their personnel ("Have a nice day"), the prospect of exchanging public bureaucrats for private entrepreneurs may be less than inspiring. But of course the presumption must be that in matters of taste, as in all else, consumer demand will not go unmet; even the most discriminating snobs will be able to purchase satisfactory service, provided they are willing to pay the price.

Practicality is a far more serious consideration. Anarcho-capitalists anticipate a skeptical audience and know they must defend themselves against the charge of being unrealistic or utopian. Often they respond by pointing out that some "government" services, such as garbage collection and even fire protection, are already provided by private entrepreneurs, though many times they are employed not by individual consumers but by municipal governments.[15] The next step is to suggest expanding this practice to more government services, such as education, land management, public recreation, and the various forms of social insurance.[16] The logic employed is always the same: private entrepreneurs will provide better service and a broader menu of consumer choices, all at a better price than government does.

The argument has begun to sound unorthodox. Sell the streets? Yes, says David Friedman, and charge drivers to gain access. Variable pricing to discourage use at times of peak demand would eliminate rush-hour traffic jams.[17] Rothbard elaborates on the proposal. He envisions two possible types of street ownership in residential neighborhoods.

> In one type, all the landowners in a certain block might become the joint *owners* of that block, let us say the "85th St. Block Company." This company would provide police protection, the costs being paid either by the homeowners directly or out of tenants' rent if the street includes rental apartments. . . .
>
> Another type of private street-ownership . . . might be private street companies, which would own only the streets, not the houses or buildings on them. The street companies would then charge landowners for the service of maintaining, improving, and policing their streets.

In the former instance, "homeowners will of course have a direct interest in seeing that their block is safe, while landlords will try to attract tenants by supplying safe streets in addition to the more usual services such as heat, water, and janitorial service." In the latter, "the street-owning companies will do their best to provide efficient street service, including police protection, to secure happy users; they will be driven to do this by their desire to make profits and to increase the value of their capital, and by their equally active desire not to suffer losses and erosion of their capital."[18] Hence private ownership and market incentives will result in better-kept and safer streets.

Here it might be objected that the elimination of public places would allow private discrimination to flourish. Rothbard concedes the point. Under anarchocapitalism, everyone would be free to discriminate, "in the sense of choosing favorably or unfavorably in accordance with whatever criteria a person may employ."[19] He insists, however, that such discrimination would be costly. The profit motive, it seems, is a great equalizer. At least, it would be among people who were more interested in enlarging their profits than in indulging their prejudices.

Finally, would not privately owned streets result in chaos in the roads if traffic symbols and regulations varied from block to block, as they might? The problem is not likely to arise, in Rothbard's view.

> The private railroads in nineteenth-century America faced similar problems and solved them harmoniously and without difficulty. Railroads allowed each other's cars on the tracks; they inter-connected with each other for mutual benefit; the gauges of the different railroads were adjusted to be uniform; and uniform freight classifications were worked out for 6,000 items. [20]

He expects no less economic rationality on the part of street owners.

The most radically unorthodox anarchocapitalist proposal is for privatizing the means of coercion and adjudication. Behind this proposal lies the Lockean proposition that in the state of nature every person has a right to execute the law of nature and to be the judge of a neighbor's transgression. [21] The anarchocapitalist merely suggests the superior convenience of hiring a professional firm to execute this right on your behalf. David Friedman points out that such firms already exist.

> Protection from coercion is an economic good. It is presently sold in a variety of forms—Brinks guards, locks, burglar alarms. As the effectiveness of government police declines, these market substitutes for the police . . . become more popular.
>
> Suppose, then, that at some future time there are no government police, but instead private protection agencies. These agencies sell the service of protecting their clients against crime. Perhaps they also guarantee their performance by insuring their clients against losses resulting from criminal acts. [22]

Rothbard commends to our attention the greater flexibility of this arrangement over government-supplied police. "On the free market, protection would be supplied in proportion and in what-

ever way consumers wish to pay for it." Moreover, he claims
that policemen dependent on the goodwill of their clients are
likely to be more courteous as well as more efficient than their
government counterparts. Arrogance and inefficiency endanger
profits.[23]

The importance of the profit motive to this system leads Rothbard himself to ask who will protect those persons too poor to
afford even the least degree of professional protection. He clearly
understands the significance of his question, for he notes that the
same problem applies to any commodity or service in the anarchocapitalist society. In light of his awareness, the answer he
gives is less than satisfying. "Very poor people," he writes,
"would be supplied, in general, by private charity."[24] Yet he
gives us no reason to believe that economic men will be charitable. Equally unsatisfying is his assertion that protection agencies
would probably offer their services without charge to the indi-
gent as a measure of goodwill. Certainly it is conceivable that
some people and some agencies will be philanthropic. But in a
system designed to secure the life and property of each person,
how can it be deemed acceptable to leave the protection of even
one individual to the charitable whims of another? On this point,
anarchocapitalism begins to sound like "anarchism for the rich."

The most serious objection anticipated by the anarchocapitalist
concerns the possibility of warfare between rival protection
agencies. Contemplating the outbreak of such warfare, Rothbard
consoles us with the observation that the hostilities would be far
less catastrophic than war between nations. "Even if local police
clash continually," he explains, "there would be no more Dres-
dens, no more Hiroshimas." But in fact he does not expect any
hostilities at all.

> To put it bluntly, such wars and conflicts would be bad—very
> bad—for business. Therefore, on the free market, the police
> agencies would all see to it that there would be no clashes be-
> tween them, and that all conflicts of opinion would be ironed
> out in private courts, decided by private judges or arbitrators.[25]

The idea of a private court system is closely tied to the anarchocapitalist proposal for private protection agencies. David Friedman envisions reliance on private arbitration specified by contractual agreement with one's protection agency.[26] Rothbard agrees that arbitration could dispose of most civil cases, and he points to the success of the American Arbitration Society to illustrate his claim. But Rothbard insists that criminal cases will require a court system, and he foresees the establishment of private courts, perhaps attached to the protection agencies, that would mete out justice according to a libertarian code of laws.* While Rothbard does not attempt to spell out this code in detail, he states that it would be based on the nonaggression axiom, with property rights defined in accordance with that principle. It would also establish rules of procedure and a schedule of punishments for any particular crime.[27] Presumably the code would evolve from contractual agreements among the various private courts, which would see it as in their best interests to arrive at some measure of uniformity.†

Private courts are the anarchocapitalist version of Locke's common judge. They allow the authoritative adjudication of disputes, however, without the need for a civil government. There is no monopoly on justice in this system, for the courts and the protection agencies are free to promulgate and enforce any "laws" they wish. Economic rationality and not state coercion produces the common framework in which a peaceful resolution of conflict is possible. If court *A* finds for the plaintiff, the defendant may take the case to court *B* in the hope of having the verdict overturned. If court *B* then finds for the defendant, the plaintiff may demand an appeal to yet a third court. Eventually the route for appeals will be cut off by an agreement among the courts themselves to limit the number of appeals in any one

---

*Rothbard never seriously considers the possibility of a nonlibertarian code of laws. But what if a market demand for some such code should arise? His own logic suggests the inevitable appearance of a justice-dealing entrepreneur to meet the demand, however draconian that justice might be.

†Rothbard sees the common law as a spontaneous growth of this sort, and he hopes to base the libertarian code on common law principles insofar as they are compatible with the nonaggression axiom. See Rothbard, *For a New Liberty*.

case.[28] Plaintiffs and defendants will accept the verdicts of these courts because they themselves have initiated the process. Their consent to be judged is part of the contract. To abrogate the contract is to place oneself in a state of war with the other parties, and they may rightly seek to enforce the verdict by coercive means. Acknowledging that right, no protection agency is likely to give aid to the rebel. But if one did, the other agencies, recognizing a threat to their system (and to their profits), would combine to shut down the outlaw by force.[29]

Philosopher Robert Nozick, himself a libertarian, has drawn the fire of anarchocapitalists for arguing that a system of competing protection agencies and private courts would logically evolve into a minimal state. According to Nozick's "invisible hand" explanation, the competition among protection agencies would result in the dominance of one agency within a given territory. Why? Because

> unlike other goods that are comparatively evaluated, maximal competing protective services cannot coexist; the nature of the service brings different agencies not only into competition for customers' patronage, but also into violent conflict with each other. [Thus] out of anarchy, pressed by spontaneous groupings, mutual-protective associations, division of labor, market pressures, economies of scale, and rational self-interest there arises something very much resembling a minimal state or a group of geographically distinct minimal states.[30]

Actually, Nozick's account has the dominant protection agency first become an "ultraminimal state," distinguished from the minimal state by the fact that its services are available only to those who purchase them. The minimal state, on the other hand, imposes its services on all persons within its territory.[31] The transition from the ultraminimal to the minimal state requires a moral justification that is both subtle and complex. In brief, we are asked to agree that because the dominant protection agency enjoys a monopoly, it "is morally required to compensate for the disadvantages it imposes upon those it prohibits from self-help activities against its clients."[32] Since "the least expensive way to compensate the independents would be to *supply* them with protective services to cover those situations of conflict with the paying customers of the protective agency," the ultraminimal state is morally required to transform itself into a minimal state.[33]

The anarchocapitalists respond first by disputing Nozick's assertion regarding the incompatibility of competing protection agencies. Roy Childs, writing in Rothbard's *Journal of Libertarian Studies,* objects to Nozick's argument by claiming that, were violent disputes to arise between agencies, " economics gives us every reason to assume that it will be more in the interest of competing parties to develop a means of arbitrating disputes rather than to engage in violent action."[34] Further objections center on Nozick's "principle of compensation," which requires that "people be compensated for having certain risky activities prohibited to them."[35] It is this principle that obliges the ultraminimal state to extend its protection to nonsubscribers. The anarchocapitalist finds unjustifiable Nozick's insistence that the dominant protection agency be allowed to assess the risk posed to its clients by the methods of competing agencies; moreover, the anarchocapitalist sees no reason for nonsubscribers to accept the protection of the dominant agency rather than some other form of compensation.[36]

Ostensibly Nozick and the anarchocapitalists share the same objective: the preservation of individual rights from wrongful invasion. At bottom, Nozick's objections to anarchism are pragmatic. He is led to the minimal state in pursuit of individual rights, not in spite of them. The anarchocapitalists, however, regard his avenue of pursuit as a retreat. They accuse him of having compromised the inviolability of individual rights in a dubious attempt to secure them from harm. Their attacks on Nozick are all the more heated because, philosophically, they are working the same side of the street. Nozick's utopia of independent city-states organized according to the preferences of their inhabitants seems almost a variant of the anarchocapitalist system.[37]*

*Nozick's utopia is really what he himself describes as a framework for utopia. It involves a free market of sorts in political systems. Presumably people

A further pragmatic objection to anarchocapitalism is voiced most strongly by critics on the right, who want to know how this society will be defended against foreign aggression.[38] David Friedman recognizes this as a hard problem, because the defense of an entire society is a public good. As Friedman explains, a public good "is an economic good which, by its nature, cannot be provided separately to each individual, but must be provided, or not provided, to all the members of a preexisting group."[39] The problem is as follows: If the nuclear missiles owned by Jones serve to deter a nuclear attack by a hostile power, then the entire community benefits, whether or not anyone but Jones has contributed to the cost of the missiles. In fact, as long as Jones is willing to bear the entire cost himself, no one else has any incentive to contribute a penny. Unfortunately, while the cost of defense is high (nuclear missiles and the like do not come cheap), the perceived value of defense is relatively low (an attack by a hostile power is not a sure thing). Given the priorities of economic men, they are not likely to fund the cost of society's defense voluntarily. Friedman's solution, not likely to please the hard-liners at the *National Review,* is to rely on private charity.[40] Rothbard, for his part, seems to be inclined to regard society's defense as a nonproblem. He initially suggests that an anarchocapitalist society would present no threat to any other society, whatever its politics, and so would not require a defensive force. Granting the possibility of an irrationally hostile neighbor, however, he maintains that alarmed consumers (though not necessarily the entire population) would purchase defensive means as they chose. Should this free market in defense prove inade-

---

will be able to choose among a variety of city-states with different constitutions. The variety of city-states available will be limited only by citizen/ consumer preferences. Of course, this utopian framework ignores the problem of child rearing and socialization. Nozick's utopian citizen/consumers are like the inhabitants of Locke's state of nature. They exist outside of history, untouched by the past, and have no allegiance to any historical state, people, or system of ideas. Real people must cope with the accumulated prejudices of the past, with affections and hatreds, with allegiances and loyalties, with conscience and ideology. Their political choices and their perception of the options never occur in a vacuum.

quate to the task and the country be occupied, he is confident that guerrilla warfare would soon drive out the invaders.[41]

The State of Nature Revisited

Locke employed the state of nature as a philosophical device for reconstructing politics. It afforded him a political *tabula rasa* unmarked by the historical record. Given nature as a social environment, Locke was able to fashion his politics of consent as an alternative to the personal rule of the father and his counterpart, the tyrant-thief. He reduced the sovereign's status to a mere shadow of its former self, making the sovereign an entity without a will of its own in an attempt to insulate the state from political motives. The political realm was transformed into a formal, legalistic framework surrounding the private world of economic men. The state, best symbolized by the hangman and the judge, was to serve as the guarantor of that private world and nothing more.

But there was an ambiguity in Locke's experiment. His politics of consent unfolded in the first state of nature, before the invention of money, when humankind shared the earth and a rough equality of condition prevailed. Under those conditions there was no need of government, for, as right and convenience went together, people were inclined to observe the rational precepts of natural law. It was only after inequality had been introduced into nature that some people had incentive to become thieves, giving their victims and potential victims good reason to seek the shelter of civil society. Yet under these conditions, the politics of consent seem unworkable. As Rousseau might observe, Lockean politics has become a clever trap set by the rich for the poor.[42]* It is not clear, however, how the trap could be sprung.

*Of the origin of government, Rousseau writes in the *Second Discourse:*

Destitute of valid reasons to justify and sufficient strength to defend himself, able to crush individuals with ease, but easily crushed himself by

The anarchists who follow in Locke's footsteps appear to be fascinated by the vision of social harmony that emerges from the first state of nature. Godwin and Spooner, each in his own way, attempt to realize that promise of social harmony by recreating the rough equality of condition that characterized nature before the invention of money. Implicitly, they become critics of modern capitalism and champions of the Jeffersonian ideal of the autonomous individual—the independent yeoman and the self-employed mechanic. Theirs is a vision of a self-regulating community of economic men secure from thieves and from the tyrant-thief. But they make no provision to protect this community from the effects of the political motives that haunt Locke's state of nature. Political ends beyond the imagination of economic men are not eradicated, merely ignored.

The anarchocapitalists return to Locke in that they embrace his second state of nature. But they reject his use of the state to guarantee order in the face of inequality. Instead they choose to remain in the state of nature, allowing the means of coercion and adjudication to remain with each individual and looking to the marketplace to provide a "common judge." For them anarchy is a moral imperative; only the formal freedom of economic exchange can ensure that social relations will be purely voluntary. They see the creation of an anarchist society as a technical problem, not a political one. Recognizing only economic motives and economic ends, they have lost sight of the very problem Locke set about to overcome. In this sense anarchocapitalism is less an escape from the threat (and promise) of politics than an escapist retreat from political life.

---

a troop of bandits, one against all, and incapable, on account of mutual jealousy, of joining with his equals against numerous enemies united by the common hope of plunder, the rich man, thus urged by necessity, conceived at length the profoundest plan that ever entered the mind of man: this was to employ in his favour the forces of those who attacked him, to make allies of his adversaries, to inspire them with different maxims, and to give them other institutions as favourable to himself as the law of nature was unfavourable. [*The Social Contract and Discourses*, trans. G. D. H. Cole (New York: E. P. Dutton, 1950), p. 250]

6

Minarchy: The Libertarian
Case for the Minimal State

The great and *chief* end . . . of Mens uniting into Common-
wealths, and putting themselves under Government, *is the Preservation of their Property*.
— JOHN LOCKE, *The Second Treatise of Government*

THE great rift in libertarian ranks is between anarchists and
minarchists. The latter, though no less energetic in their defense
of individual rights and personal freedom, reject anarchocapitalism as being unworkable and call instead for a return to the
minimal night–watchman state of classical liberal theory. Because
minarchy is more easily identified with conventional liberal ideas,
it may at first glance seem less radical, or simply less fanciful, than
libertarian anarchism. Perhaps for this reason it has received more
serious scholarly attention. Robert Nozick's minarchist tract, *Anarchy, State, and Utopia* (to pick the most celebrated example), is
widely regarded as one of the most important contemporary
works of political philosophy. Minarchy is more politically palat-
able as well; after all, devotion to the concept of minimal government ("that government is best which governs least") lies close to
the heart of the American political tradition. It seems safe to
conclude that minarchy is far more likely to find an audience
among the general public than anarchy.

Yet minarchists no less than anarchocapitalists seek to effect a
radical transformation of American politics and society. Unlike
those contemporary politicians who invoke the minimal state as
a catch phrase in their rhetorical assault on "bloated" government bureaucracies, minarchists advance the idea of a minimal

state as a guiding principle admitting no room for compromise. Their aim is permanently to restrict the scope of governmental operations, reducing the modern state to the role of Locke's "common judge with authority" to promulgate laws (for the protection of property), punish thieves and other malefactors, and defend the nation against foreign aggressors. The free society this minimal government is to serve will derive its contours from the uninhibited play of market forces. Minarchists boldly and insistently proclaim the unity of capitalism and freedom. They place great store in the technical efficiency and also the moral fitness of the capitalist economy, and deem themselves among its last defenders in a world nearly overcome by collectivist fancies.

Like Nozick, a great number of the minarchist authors are professional philosophers.* It comes as something of a surprise, therefore, to discover the relative poverty of minarchist theory. The whole body of minarchist literature provides no new argument for the minimal state; it merely rehearses and perhaps reaffirms arguments long familiar to students of classical liberalism. From an academic standpoint, minarchy seems to be a belated defense of ideas that were already stale more than a century ago. So, too, the minarchist apology for capitalism, given in the language of Adam Smith and Horatio Alger, seems oddly inappropriate to an age of bureaucratic management and multinational corporations. Ironically, minarchy appears radical because it is anachronistic.

The Ideology of the Minimal State

Libertarian theory starts with an assertion of inviolable individual rights. This avowal in itself is ideologically unexceptional given the cultural milieu in which libertarians write. What distinguishes the libertarian defenders of the minimal state is the

---

*The list of minarchists includes John Hospers, Tibor Machan, Eric Mack, and Lansing Pollock, all of whom make their living as professors of philosophy.

closed system they develop from this original assertion. Minarchy is more than a theory of government; it is a statement of the (one) morally correct political order. From the premise that all persons have an equal right to life, liberty, and property, minarchists derive the moral necessity of the miminal state, the immorality of the positive state, and the moral fitness of social relations that grow out of capitalist exchange.

It is evidence of the sectarian character of the libertarian movement that the first minarchist salvo is directed not at the positive state but against libertarian anarchists. (An enemy within one's own camp always seems to be the more immediate danger.) The anarchists, of course, are equally committed to the doctrine of individual rights; in fact, as we have seen, they abandoned the classical liberal idea of government only when they were unable to reconcile the enjoyment of those rights with the coercive power of the minimal state. In the *Second Treatise* Locke asks, "If Man in the State of Nature be so free, as has been said; if he be absolute Lord of his own Person and Possessions, equal to the greatest, and subject to no Body, why will he part with his Freedom?"[1] Libertarian anarchists ask the same question and answer it by stating that no rational person would willingly compromise his freedom by accepting the yoke of government, however benign its purpose.

Locke, of course, did not find the state of nature very "convenient." With every person a judge in his own case, he envisioned justice neglected out of a concern by each for his own self-interest.[2] Following Locke, minarchists simply do not trust people to act justly or to display unbiased judgment when their interests are at stake. To leave what Locke called the "executive right of the law of nature" (the right to punish alleged transgressions of natural law) in private hands would be to invite chaos. "If a society left the retaliatory use of force in the hands of individual citizens," writes Ayn Rand, "it would degenerate into mob rule, lynch law and an endless series of bloody feuds or vendettas."[3] Minarchists insist that there must be a Lockean common judge with authority if there is to be a peaceful resolution of disputes within the community. John Hospers argues at some length that the anarchocapitalist scheme for the provision of police and court services through private "protective agencies" is impractical. Like Robert Nozick, he is haunted by the grim specter of incessant warfare among competing suppliers.[4]

At first glance, the minarchist objection to anarchocapitalism seems eminently reasonable. After all, in the absence of a mutually recognized authority, how would hostile individuals reconcile their differences? Why should either one abandon his claim if he thought his the just cause and believed he might yet prevail, by force of arms if not by persuasion? But perhaps we concede too much by accepting the example of a dispute in progress (and a violent one at that). For their part, libertarian anarchists maintain that rational individuals are likely to choose reasonable ways of resolving their differences, preferring an orderly process involving arbitration by a neutral third party to the disorder and greater uncertainty of self-enforcement.[5] Why do minarchists come to the opposite conclusion?

The only answer we can discern in the structure of their argument is that human nature will not allow such optimism. Self-interest, or more plainly selfishness, renders human society prone to conflict. As was mentioned earlier, this view has its roots in Locke's *Second Treatise*. It is worth noting as a gloss on the libertarian argument, however, that Locke does not ascribe the origin of the state to natural human contentiousness. In fact, Locke's hypothetical account of original government has much more to do with the social and economic conditions in which the parties to the social compact find themselves than it does with human nature. Locke's account begins in the state of nature, an anarchic situation that is a state of peace and shared abundance before the invention of money. Government is hardly missed in this (first) state of nature because rational, self-interested individuals have no incentive to break natural law. More specifically, the distribution of wealth (which is roughly equal) presents no occasion for any quarrel. This situation changes with the invention of money, which creates a nonperishable form of wealth (as distinguished from the fruits of nature) and allows the free exercise of individual rights (expressly the right of property) to generate a structure of inequality previously unknown in the world. In this (second) state of nature, where the common stock has been transformed into relatively few private holdings, some people will have reason enough to steal. It is at this point that government becomes necessary for the maintenance of order and the protection of individual rights.

Locke's argument might be restated as follows. Given a rough equality of condition, anarchy is at least possible. Absent this equality, human nature will incline toward conflicts of interest that render government indispensable. Of course, it is not merely equality that makes for social peace in Locke's account, but the impossibility of inequality. Locke fully expects that differences among individuals will lead some to be more industrious, and more successful, than others. The shift from natural wealth (ownership of perishable goods) to money (nonperishable wealth) allows industrious individuals to expand the size of their holdings beyond that for which they have immediate use and forever extinguishes the primitive equality of nature. Locke's history of property leads from natural abundance to artificial scarcity. Civil society is introduced as a political solution to an economic problem.

Drawing back from Locke's argument, we might do well to reflect that wealth is not the only object of human passion. Outside the state of nature, in the real world known to history, people have fought and died in the name of God, clan, country, and countless other causes far removed from their material interests. The primacy of economic motives is distinctive of the liberal tradition (though it is not unique to liberalism). Before Locke can take this motivational assumption for granted, he must remove human beings from history and place them in "nature." Three centuries later Locke's heirs have no need of this philosophic device. Themselves products of an essentially Lockean culture, minarchists take Locke's psychology as given. It seems natural for them to conceive of human beings in the spirit of C. B. Macpherson's "possessive individualism," forgetting that this human type is largely a cultural artifact.[6]

In a sense, minarchists are caught up in a Hartzian paradox.

They are "irrational Lockeans" whose political experience causes them to grasp only a part of Locke's teaching. Having no historical politics they wish to repudiate (no feudalism, no feudal legacy), they miss the significance of Locke's natural history in the *Second Treatise* and build their view of the state on the rock of his psychology. Indeed, "human nature" does provide a Lockean rationale for government, provided we assume conditions of inequality and the primacy of economic motives among self-interested individuals. As Louis Hartz points out, it has never been difficult for Americans to make these assumptions, because in large measure they are true of the American experience.[7] The danger here is that the particulars of the American experience will be mistaken for universal truths.

If persons in the state of nature (or with a state-of-nature mentality) have no sense of history, they have equally little awareness of class. The irony in Locke's account of original government is that the means devised to secure property rights in the face of socially disruptive inequality will, as a matter of course, perpetuate the very conditions that render spontaneous adherence to natural law improbable. The state, acting "impartially" to guarantee individual rights, ends up serving the interests of a particular class. This irony is lost on the libertarians, whose notion of political reality conforms almost perfectly to the state of nature. They readily accept the liberal concept of the state as a class-neutral third party. Their naiveté is hardly surprising. Only if one stands outside the state of nature (history is a good vantage point) is one able to see the liberal state as an instrument of class rule. The failure of minarchists to discern the bias of the liberal state is owed partly to their inability to recognize class antagonisms. In this matter they appear to be truly blind and not merely obstinate. Locked into a state-of-nature mentality, minarchists identify the liberal personality with human nature itself. Social atomism is taken to be the natural condition of humankind. In such a bourgeois universe it is not surprising to discover a lack of self-awareness among bourgeois ideologues.

Their state-of-nature mentality also helps to explain why minarchists devote the greater part of their theorizing to the relationship between the individual and the state. As "irrational Lockeans," they take the purposes of civil society for granted. There is no question as to the proper role of the state; it exists to protect the free exercise of inviolable individual rights. To do so, however, the state must have the power to coerce malefactors. The use of coercion raises two problems. First, what legitimates the use of force by government? And second, what will prevent the illegitimate use of force against honest citizens? The answer to these questions form the basis for the disagreement between minarchists and anarchocapitalists.

Generally, minarchists find a moral justification for state power in some variation of Locke's argument from consent. Locke argues that civil society comes into being through the agreement of its founders "to joyn and unite into a Community." After the founding, no person can be considered a member of society who does not expressly consent to membership. Once given, this declaration of consent may not be taken back; only the dissolution of government returns the individual to the state of nature. Upon entering civil society each individual surrenders to government two powers that all enjoyed in nature: the power to do whatever was necessary to ensure their preservation and the power to judge and punish violations of natural law. In return the government is obliged to protect their lives and property through the promulgation and impartial enforcement of uniform laws "directed to no other *end*, but the *Peace, Safety,* and *publick good* of the People."[8]

According to Locke, the original compact establishes "one *Body Politick,* wherein the *Majority* have a Right to act and conclude the rest." In defense of majority rule Locke offers first a pragmatic justification, arguing that society cannot long survive unless its members can be required to act in concert. Employing a physical analogy, he writes that "it is necessary to that which is one body to move in one way." The body politic "should move that way whither the greater force carries it, which is the consent of the majority." A further pragmatic consideration is the improbability of achieving unanimous consent on every issue given "the variety of Opinions, and contrariety of Interests, which unavoidably happen in all Collections of Men." But Locke also places majority rule within the moral compass of the consent argument. He requires that the original compact contain a clause obliging each member of society to be bound by the will of the majority in all subsequent measures.[9] Hence, technically speaking, the individual in society freely consents even to those policies he may find objectionable.

Persons who reside among the community but are not themselves members (i.e., have not given their consent) must still obey the laws of the majority. Locke argues that any person who enjoys the protection of the laws has, in effect, given tacit consent to their enforcement. Merely by entering the government's territorial jurisdiction the individual is obliged to accept its rightful authority.[10] Unlike a declaration of express consent, however, this acceptance does not bind the individual in perpetuity. Sojourners may quit the territory when they please. Still, they pay a price for this freedom in not having a say in the legislature. The doctrine of tacit consent allows Locke to establish the legitimacy of state actions affecting persons who are in but not of civil society. This doctrine prevents any individual from escaping the "inconveniences" of nature without coming under the authority of government.

Such minarchists as John Hospers and Tibor Machan tend to emphasize the importance of express consent. Both men have written books intended to persuade the reader that the minarchist conception of government deserves the allegiance of all rational persons. Their common argument may be summarized as follows. Rational individuals will accept the validity of libertarian principles once these principles are explained and the fallacies of collectivism laid bare. Having been brought to a realization of the truth, rational persons *ought* to become libertarians. (Failure to act on the truth indicates either a lack of rationality or an evil will.) Persons committed to libertarian principles will recognize the need of government to secure individual rights, and so *ought* to consent to the authority of such a government.[11] Hospers apparently finds this argument so commonsensical that he takes acceptance of its conclusion for granted. In responding to anarchocapitalist arguments he appears to assume that a government designed to minarchist specifications will automatically enjoy the consent of the governed.[12]

From the anarchist perspective, Hospers' assumption falls flat. What if the individual withholds consent (for whatever reason)? What then legitimates the enforcement of laws, the execution of public works, and, most fundamental, the collection of taxes? In Locke's scheme, the doctrine of tacit consent places the burden of proof on the individual. Any person who accepts the protection of the laws will be thought to have accepted their legitimacy. In order to express rejection of the state's authority, dissenters must remove themselves beyond its jurisdiction. Minarchists do not employ this solution, possibly because they recognize it as a clever evasion of the issue. Like their anarchist counterparts, they believe that the individual may be coerced by others only in retaliation for an invasive act. This means that acceptance and support of government must be completely voluntary, no less so than when a consumer freely patronizes some business.

The difficulty introduced by the consent requirement is most acutely felt in regard to taxes. In their attempts to escape the problem of compulsory taxation, minarchists are driven to proposing schemes for the provision of government services on a fee-for-service basis.[13] Reliance on voluntary contributions and service charges, however, will not solve the problem of collective goods. Either these sorts of goods (such as national defense) must be done without or the government must be allowed forcibly to extract the necessary funds from unwilling citizens. The latter course cannot sit easily with the likes of Tibor Machan, who finds it necessary to derive even the authority to punish criminals from their own consent.*

Robert Nozick is one minarchist who does not take legitimacy for granted. Perhaps because he recognizes the difficulties inherent in the consent formula, he attempts to show that the minimal state could arise spontaneously, without a Lockean original com-

---

*Machan argues that because criminals give their consent to the law, they also consent to the penalties attached to breaking the law (*Human Rights and Human Liberties* [Chicago: Nelson Hall, 1975], pp. 115–16).

pact. Nozick begins with a hypothetical state of nature in which individuals are free to purchase police and judicial services from any number of competing "protective agencies." This anarchic original condition does not last long, however. The very nature of protective services inevitably brings the competing agencies into violent conflict, and in due course competition gives way to a de facto territorial monopoly exercised by the strongest or dominant agency. Nozick characterizes the dominant protective agency as an "ultraminimal state," distinguished from the minimal state by the fact that not all persons within its territorial jurisdiction are its clients; independents are still at liberty to enforce their (natural) rights as they see fit and have no claim upon the services of the dominant agency. The minimal state comes into being when independents are prohibited from enforcing their claims against agency clients (because the agency deems their procedures unreliable) and, in compensation, are offered the agency's services (free or at a reduced fee) in settling their disputes with its paying customers.[14]

While Nozick is sensitive to the need for moral justification, his "invisible hand" explanation of the state's origins does not fully resolve the problem of legitimacy. As his critics among the anarchocapitalists point out, the legitimacy of Nozick's state rests on two dubitable (if not dubious) propositions. The first is Nozick's claim that a de facto territorial monopoly is the necessary outcome of a competition among protective agencies. On the assumption that such a competition would prove harmonious, there is no need to venture beyond the hypothetical state of nature. Yet this objection need not detain us if we are willing to grant the mere plausibility of Nozick's claim. A de facto monopoly, should one come into being, does not violate libertarian constraints in that nothing prevents potential competitors from entering the market. Nor is the dominant agency in violation of anyone's rights by refusing to cooperate with its would-be competitors; nothing requires the dominant agency to consider valid any but its own procedures (and its own administration of those procedures).[15] As long as the agency does not force anyone to accept its services, its statelike role is morally unobjectionable.

More troublesome is Nozick's claim that independents may be prohibited from enforcing their rights against agency clients provided they are offered the agency's protection in compensation. Nozick's anarchocapitalist critics see this as a rather lame excuse for imposing the state on those who do not want it.[16] Actually, Nozick does not insist that independents must accept the agency's offer of compensation (though it is clearly in their interests to do so), nor does he give the newly emerged minimal state authority to meddle in disputes between independents (a restriction he views as providing independents with an additional incentive to purchase the state's protection). Hence he cannot be said to impose government on those who will not have it. In effect, what Nozick does is to create circumstances under which most persons can be expected to accept the minimal state of their own accord. Yet the fact remains that he allows the state to prohibit certain "risky" activities without first obtaining the consent of those affected by the prohibition. This measure is difficult to square with the minarchist commitment to inviolable individual rights.

Why does Nozick insist on prohibiting self-help enforcement of their rights by independents? Could not the state judge each enforcement action by an independent on a case-by-case basis, permitting to stand those it finds to be just while exacting compensation and inflicting punishment for those it determines to have been wrongful? How does faulty enforcement by an independent differ from any other wrongful act, such as breach of contract? For Nozick there is a difference, and a significant one. Unlike breach of contract, self-help enforcement (when carried out in error) belongs to a class of wrongs that have a public component. Such wrongs, according to Nozick, create fear among the general public even though people know they will be compensated fully if and when the wrongs occur. "Even under the strongest compensation proposal which compensates victims for their fear [as well as for the injury suffered], some people (the nonvictims) will not be compensated for *their* fear."[17] For this reason self-help enforcement by independents, which is a risky activity (it might be carried out in error), induces a state of general anxiety that can be relieved only by prohibition of the risky activity.

On the other hand, Nozick assumes that it is possible to compensate independents for what they are forced to give up. Under Nozick's principle of compensation, no great harm is done to independents if what they are offered in compensation by the state leaves them no worse off than they would have been were they allowed to enforce their rights on their own. At the same time, this requirement imposes no undue redistributive burden on paying clients of the state (who now share the cost of protecting the independents), because they are morally obligated to compensate those persons denied the right of self-help enforcement.[18] (The obligation arises from the fact that self-help enforcement is merely risky and not necessarily wrongful. Were it clearly a wrongful act, say like theft, compensation would not need to accompany prohibition.)

This argument presents a significant modification of the minarchist position. In the first place, it claims that rights may be abridged under certain circumstances provided there is adequate compensation. Second, it claims that the state may legitimately determine when these circumstances obtain as well as what constitutes adequate compensation. Finally, it justifies the state's action not on the occurrence of an actual injury but on the assessed risk of such injury. The significance of the last point becomes clear if we compare the prohibition of self-help enforcement with the prohibition of theft. Theft certainly seems an example of what Nozick calls a public wrong. Although any particular theft affects only some particular victim or victims, the fear of theft can easily haunt the public and induce free-floating anxiety.[19] Yet theft is outlawed not on account of the worry it generates but because it is a wrongful invasion of property rights. Self-help enforcement, on the other hand, can be generally prohibited not because it is wrong (it is merely risky) but only because it makes for a climate of anxiety which the community is justified in seeking to avoid.

Nozick states that the prohibition of public wrongs is in the "public interest."[20] What remains unclear is the sense in which

Nozick is able to rely on the public interest as a justification for state action. The problem here is that his concept of civil society leaves no room for a political community in Locke's sense of "the Body Politick." In Locke's account, the public interest is simply the interest agreed upon by a numerical majority, subject to certain constitutional restraints. But Nozick's state is not responsible to its clients in the Lockean sense, for it is not a political creation. On the contrary, it is a private entity free to frame its "laws" as it sees fit. Presumably its desire to attract and keep paying customers will lead to the promulgation of laws that are generally popular (though not popularly approved). Still, its de facto monopoly may well give us cause to worry on that score. In any event, it is hard to see how Nozick is able to speak of a public in any meaningful sense of that term given the absence of a political community. As it stands, his "public interest" is in danger of becoming whatever the state says it is.

This outcome is ironic, for Nozick seeks to abolish politics in order to prevent the (democratic) state from acting tyranically. Like other minarchists, he has little faith in most persons' inclination to respect individual rights. Yet, as is true of the minarchist enterprise generally, his argument founders on the attempt to construct a state without politics. It is characteristic of minarchist thought to treat the minimal state as though it really were nothing other than the dominant protective agency. So long as this fiction is maintained (and not studied too closely), the problem of consent vanishes, for citizens are transformed into clients; politics is not so much transcended as swallowed up by the market. The problem of consent reemerges, however, once we stop to consider the relationship between the state and nonclients. At this point the state can preserve its legitimacy only by deviating from a strict regard for individual rights (as Nozick does). The problem here is that minarchists lack a justifiable rationale for restricting anyone's rights (unless, of course, the victims of state action are themselves proven aggressors).

The singular advantage of Locke's original compact is that it creates a political rationale for state action that does not jeopardize the legitimacy of the state. Within the Lockean argument, every constitutionally valid state action is, in effect, authored by the people, for the government (whatever its institutional form) is their creature. Perhaps minarchists are frightened by this argument because they associate representative government with modern democracy, which they identify with limitless state power. But of course Locke was no democrat and his argument need not be viewed as a slippery slope leading to unlimited democracy. It is likely that Locke imagined the political community as a select group committed to the preservation of individual rights. Once established, this bourgeois civil society might demand conformity from a reactionary aristocracy and a revolutionary proletariat via the doctrine of tacit consent. In seeking to improve on Locke, the minarchists deny themselves Locke's own defense against a democratic politics.

Beyond the problem of legitimacy the minarchist faces the problem of keeping the minimal state within its rightful authority. Even the minimal state, because it enjoys a monopoly on the (legitimate) use of force, is a potential tyrant. Anarchocapitalists rely on the presence of competing protective agencies to curb the lust for power. It is supposed that if one agency should turn outlaw, the others would quickly move to preserve the good order of the market by liquidating the rogue.[21] Anarchists criticize their erstwhile minarchist allies for naively rejecting the only truly effective check on state power. For their part, minarchists again prefer a more conventional Lockean solution. Following Locke and self-consciously treading the path worn by the authors of the United States Constitution, they suggest hemming in the state with strict constitutional provisions that define the extent of governmental authority. Tyranny is to be forever banished by the rule of law.[22] And behind the law, adding strength to the paper barricades of constitutionalism, they place the Lockean right of revolution. A lawless government abrogates the social compact.[23]

Still, all in all, minarchists display what seems surprisingly little concern over the potential for abuse of state power. When Tibor Machan discusses the right of revolution, it is not to establish a check on the minimal state but to explain how far the citizens of existing states may go to establish a libertarian regime. (He counsels violence only as a last resort.)[24] On contemplating the minarchists' apparent confidence in the benign intentions of the minimal state, one is tempted to wonder what ever became of the dour view of human nature that provides the rationale for government in the first place. The minarchist state resembles nothing so much as Locke's "phantom sovereign," a creature without a will (or interests) of its own.[25] This phantom would not frighten even the most timid opponent of statism. What is there to fear from the ghost of the state? But then, ghosts do not reach beyond the grave to impose taxes or imprison the living. The minarchist state is not dead or even greatly diminished in strength. It retains control over the means of coercion and employs them for particular purposes.

If minarchists do not fear the use of state power, it is because they approve of the state's objectives. The reason for this approval is easy enough to understand. Simply put, the minimal state exists to protect the rights of property. The fact that minarchists describe this right as fundamental and universal[26] cannot disguise the partisan role of the state in a world characterized by substantial inequality. To the propertied classes the state that serves their interests must indeed appear to be a mere phantom, its presence hardly felt at all; to the propertyless, however, the state must seem much more a thing of substance and terror.*

It is highly revealing of the minarchists' true concerns that they make no defense of traditional civil liberties. One might well expect people worried about the protection of individual liberty to insist on stringent constitutional safeguards to ensure the citizen's freedom of speech and assembly, the right to vote, and so

---

*Consider public attitudes toward the police. Middle-class persons tend to view the police as public servants, though occasionally irksome ones. (Witness the ire of the businessman given a speeding ticket on his way home from the office.) Working-class persons and the poor tend toward a more hostile view. They often regard the police as disciplinarians; at worst, in urban ghettos, the police are looked on as an army of occupation. See *Report of the National Advisory Commission on Civil Disorders* (Washington, D.C.: U.S. Government Printing Office, 1968), especially chap. 11.

on. Yet no such measures are urged by minarchists. On the contrary, these very civil rights are effectively stripped of all protection by the minarchists' focus on property rights, which are said to be the origin (and the limit) of all human rights. The minarchist claim is that by preserving the rights of property we vouchsafe all other (subsidiary) rights. In John Hospers' illustration of this point, the right of free speech becomes the right to speak one's mind on one's own property or on another's property rented for the occasion.[27] The state may not abridge freedom of speech precisely because it has no authority to interfere with the lawful use of private property. But what of the state's responsibility to prevent discrimination? Will the minimal state be permitted to take affirmative action to ensure all persons equal opportunity to speak out? In the absence of a "public space" protected by government, no such right of free speech exists. Just as in the stateless realm of anarchocapitalism, nonconformists unable to secure a podium from disapproving landlords must respect the rights of property owners and remain silent. Under minarchy, any act of trespass will invoke the power of the state against them. In their quest to vanquish political tyranny minarchists risk establishing the tyranny of property.*

Capitalism and the Good Society

In designing a government to serve their conception of human rights and liberty, minarchists shrink the public realm—the realm of collective action and collective responsibilities—until it is barely large enough to support the minimal state they desire. As the space (both social and psychic) in which to lead a public life recedes, privacy expands, turning the social world into the atomistic universe of Locke's state of nature. This scheme ex-

---

*It is not my argument that the rich will invariably oppress the poor. Rather, my aim is to suggest the possibility of intolerance and to point out the minarchists' insensitivity to this problem. The lust for profit is indeed a powerful incentive to treat all paying customers alike; but as the history of American racism makes clear, it is no substitute for a tough antidiscrimination statute.

cludes far more than the positive state. It sunders the affective ties binding individuals one to another, leaving each person perfectly free and independent of the rest. Of course, social atomism is not the end but rather the starting point of minarchist social theory. In this emotionally simplified environment free individuals can go on to build a new social order that will preserve their mutual independence and facilitate their self-interested pursuit of disparate goals. That order, the only social order compatible with human freedom as libertarians define it, is the capitalist order of a market society.

Ideologically, the minarchist defense of the minimal state is inextricably linked to an apology for capitalism. Since, in the name of human rights and personal liberty, the state will not be allowed to alter market outcomes, it is of critical importance that these outcomes be demonstrated to be just. Perhaps the most celebrated minarchist defense of capitalism is presented by Robert Nozick. Essentially, his claim is that just acquisitions and just transfers ("just" here denotes the absence of force or fraud) legitimate the distribution of wealth resulting from capitalist exchange. However well or poorly any given individual fares in this process, his or her rights remain inviolate; the general outcome, whether approved or not, is purely the result of the exercise of human liberty. Thus there is no morally coherent reason to "correct" market outcomes by redistribution of wealth.[28]

Nozick presents his argument as a theory of just entitlement. As Amy Gutmann has noted, however, his argument implies a theory of just desert. The two are not the same and will not serve equally well in defense of the market. Consider Gutmann's restatement of Nozick's Wilt Chamberlain example, intended as an illustration of entitlement:

> Let us say that each of one million fans is willing to pay 25 cents of the total admission price directly to Wilt to see him play basketball. Nozick wants us to ask, Is not Chamberlain entitled to keep his $250,000? But are we really wondering instead, on being asked this question, Does Wilt *deserve* his $250,000?[29]

Gutmann's question invites us to consider the meaning of "desert." The term refers to the *worthiness* of the individual. A reward is deserved if one has earned it by merit. Can we apply the term to the outcomes of the market process? No, not meaningfully, for prices in the free market reflect only the subjective value attached by economic actors to various goods and services. Chamberlain's $250,000 may accurately represent the market value of his appearance in any one game, but we are not justified in concluding that he is "worth" the money, or even that he has "earned" his reward. It is nothing Chamberlain does, but rather what his fans do, that determines his market value. In this sense, the market is indifferent to merit.*

Nozick may still insist that Chamberlain is nevertheless entitled to his money. Whether or not it can be said that Wilt actually deserves the $250,000, all must admit that the exchange in question is fair (i.e., no rights are violated), so no one has cause to complain. Is this not defense enough to secure the status of market outcomes? Certainly it is difficult to imagine someone in Chamberlain's position making any complaint. Yet what of the player who believes very strongly that he deserves an equal amount and receives far less? The disappointed player may well have more native ability, work harder at developing his skill, and truly play harder than his better-paid teammate, and still be valued less highly by the fans. Will he not complain of injustice? How is he to be reconciled to the indifference of the market process?

Ideologically speaking, justice is not the issue here. Rather, it is a question of what people are likely to accept as just. The popular

*It may be argued that Chamberlain's market value stems from the fans' appreciation of his skill, and so indirectly at least is a measure of his true worth. The problem with this claim is that we do not know for certain why the fans are willing to pay their 25 cents apiece to see Wilt play. They may indeed value his skills. Or perhaps they like his style on the court, his sense of humor, or even his good looks. It is conceivable that fans would pay as much to see a very poor player simply because they were entertained by his clumsiness. (Once upon a time an argument of this sort might have been used to explain the popularity of the New York Mets.) See the discussion of market value and personal merit in Friedrich Hayek, *Law, Legislation, and Liberty*, vol. 2 (Chicago: University of Chicago Press, 1976), chap. 10. Hayek's views are discussed below and again in chap. 7.

myth regarding the free market—a myth given form and rein-
forced by the Horatio Alger parables of success—is that native
ability and hard work will not go unrewarded. In this vein,
libertarian philosopher John Hospers assures us that in a capitalist
economy the individual's earnings "bear a close relation to his
effort and achievements."[30] The notion of just desert lends tremendous credibility to the market and, if accepted without question, easily serves to legitimate the distribution of wealth resulting from capitalist exchange. Collapsing the notions of just
desert and entitlement, Nozick suggests the following (admittedly unwieldy) maxim as a summary of the capitalist position:

> From each according to what he chooses to do, to each accord-
> ing to what he makes for himself (perhaps with the contracted
> aid of others) and what others choose to do for him and choose
> to give him of what they've been given previously (under this
> maxim) and haven't expended or transferred.[31]*

Unfortunately, our experience in the market does not confirm
the notion of just desert. As so staunch a friend of capitalism as
Friedrich Hayek points out, the market can be extremely arbitrary. It allows individuals to employ their skills and resources
for their own purposes and at their own discretion, yet under
circumstances neither they nor anyone else can control. Hayek
likens the market process to a game in which outcomes are dependent partly on the skill of individual players and partly on
luck. For any given player, native ability, learned skills, and, of
course, degree of effort are not without effect; but they cannot
guarantee the final outcome. Unfortunate circumstances may
still defeat the meritorious individual. And, just as fortuitously,
an undeserving competitor may win the jackpot. These are the
breaks of the game. The danger, as Hayek sees it, is that losers
who believe that they deserve to win may become disaffected
and seek to change the rules. Worried by the prospect, he toys
with discarding the Horatio Alger myth altogether. Just as he is

*Nozick immediately shortens the maxim to read: "From each as they
choose, to each as they are chosen."

about to consign it to the wastebin, however, he recalls its usefulness and hesitates, uncertain whether to give up so powerful an incentive to honest industry.[32]

Hayek is well aware that entitlement is ideologically less compelling than desert. The meritorious individual who nevertheless loses in the "game" of capitalism can hardly be expected to take comfort from the "fairness" of his loss. Hayek's response is to stress the material advantages of entrepreneurial efficiency and innovation. Asking us to acknowledge the tremendous advance in our standard of living made possible by the capitalist economy, he counsels that we had best learn to accept the occasional disappointments suffered in the market as the price of maintaining the general welfare. Further, he seeks to console the victims of ill fortune by pointing out that if capitalism presents the risk of unmerited failure, it also provides each individual an unparalleled chance at success. Finally, he admonishes losers of the capitalist game that they are better off in the free-market system, with its high overall standard of living, than they could ever hope to be in a socialist economy.[33]*

Hayek's argument comes close to abandoning all moral pretentions. Capitalism is deemed "good" because it is efficient at generating wealth. If we simply leave off any claims concerning individual rights, including the right to liberty, Hayek's apology

---

*In *The Constitution of Liberty* (Chicago: University of Chicago Press, 1960), chap. 3, Hayek claims to be in basic agreement with John Rawls's argument in *A Theory of Justice* (Cambridge: Harvard University Press, 1971). According to Rawls, inequality within a framework of institutions required by equal liberty and fair equality of opportunity is just "if and only if [the higher expectations of those better situated] work as part of a scheme which improves the expectations of the least advantaged members of society" (p. 75). Rawls calls this the difference principle. In essence, Hayek is claiming that the free market operates in accord with Rawls's difference principle. That is, the production and distribution of goods in the market cannot benefit the rich without improving the welfare of the least well-off members of society. Unlike Rawls, however, Hayek is not concerned with the justice of the market process or the resulting distribution of resources. To his mind, the market is neither just nor unjust. Lacking intentions (it is, after all, a process and not a person), it lacks moral qualities. See the discussion of Hayek's argument in chap. 7 below.

for capitalism comes to rest on hedonism alone.* In contrast, Tibor Machan, a disciple of Ayn Rand and a leading minarchist theoretician, is not content to rest the defense of capitalism on an appeal to its efficiency. Such a defense, he claims, is not strong enough to win the hearts and minds of the people.

> One cannot ultimately justify a basic human institution—a socioeconomic system—by reference to such criteria as "workable," "useful," "efficient," and so forth. Man's nature as a moral agent requires justification for his actions, institutions, and policies on the basis of what is right and good. Only *then* can we determine what will work best to achieve it, and what is most efficient or useful for that purpose.

He readily grants that capitalism is "the most efficient system of economic organization," but he contends that the defense of the free market is not complete until capitalism has been shown to serve the good—"the objective good, not just anyone's idea of it."[34]

Machan's demand adds a new dimension to the minarchist argument. Nowhere in the writings of Hayek or Nozick do we find a claim that capitalism is morally justified because it serves some unique, objective good. On the contrary, one of the things they most appreciate about capitalist society is its built-in tolerance for an incredibly wide variety of ultimate ends. Both Hayek and Nozick are perfectly indifferent to the good sought by any individual, as long as its pursuit does not require the willful violation of others' rights. In short, they believe that personal morality is a private matter and that public morality consists solely of policing individual rights.† In the absence of a societal

---

*Hayek never surrenders the moral claim, though at times he comes close to doing so. See, for example, the hymn to material progress in chap. 3 of *Constitution of Liberty*. Norman Barry classifies Hayek as a "consequentialist libertarian," concerned primarily with the instrumental value of liberty and not with its moral value. I think this claim a bit harsh, but understandable. (See Norman Barry, "The New Liberalism," *British Journal of Political Science* 13[January 1983]:93–123).

†In discussing his utopian framework, Nozick explains that libertarianism

consensus as to the nature of the good life, this (almost) any-
thing-goes philosophy is one of the more attractive features of
libertarianism. It offers a moral pluralism to match America's
cultural and ethnic pluralism. Machan is not so dogmatic a mor-
alist as to risk contradicting his libertarian beliefs by denying
"free" individuals the right to live the good life as best they
discern it. He shuns the hedonistic implications of moral rela-
tivism, however, insisting that the good life is indeed objectively
knowable. Individuals remain free to choose the good life or
some less good alternative; but, having been brought to an
awareness of the "objective good," they morally ought to
choose that way of life over any other.[35]

What does Machan mean by the good life? In his own words,
to lead the good life is to live rationally. But then we must ask:
What does it mean to live rationally, and why is rationality the
key to right action? When we seek an answer to these questions,
it is perhaps most efficient to by-pass Machan and go directly to
the source of his moral views, the writings of Ayn Rand. (This
course seems eminently fair, as Machan himself turns to Rand
whenever he wishes to illustrate a point or—even more often—to
substantiate a claim.)[36] In *The Virtue of Selfishness*, Rand explains
that life is the ultimate standard of value:

> An *ultimate* value is that final goal or end to which all lesser goals
> are the means—and it sets the standard by which all lesser goals
> are *evaluated*. An ogranism's life is its *standard of value:* that which
> furthers its life is the *good*, that which threatens it is the *evil*.[37]

The brute fact of existence, therefore, is the bedrock on which
objective morality is founded. In Rand's argument, and those of
her disciples, this proposition has the status of an indisputable

---

substitutes a "utopian process" for "utopian ends." That is, it leaves ultimate
ends undetermined out of respect for individual liberty. (See Robert Nozick,
Anarchy, State, and Utopia [New York: Basic Books, 1968], pp. 331–33; also pp.
160–64.) Hayek, for his part, is something of a moral relativist who believes
that different cultures evolve different moral rules, yet all such rules are functionally equivalent. (See *Law, Legislation, and Liberty*, 2:18–27. See also *Constitution of Liberty*, pp. 62–63.)

axiom.[38] Reason and morality are linked by the assertion that "reason is man's basic means of survival." Consequently, "that which is proper to the life of a rational being is the good; that which negates, opposes, or destroys it is the evil."[39]

Citing Aristotle as well as Rand, Machan claims reason to be the unique, defining characteristic of human beings. It follows, he argues, that to be truly human a person must exercise his rational capacity. "He must choose to live in such a way that he achieves the goals that are rational for him, individually but also as a human being."[40] Machan's argument turns on a rather muddled distinction between instrumental rationality and some vaguely presented notion of a higher rationality associated with membership in the human species. Just how we are to determine what is rational for the individual *as an individual* opposed to what is rational for the same individual *as a human being* is never made clear.

It turns out, as a practical matter, that to live rationally, and hence morally, is to live for oneself. Machan endorses Rand's prescription for ethical egoism. Their creed is that of John Galt, the hero of Rand's novel *Atlas Shrugged:* "I swear by my life and my love that I will never live for the sake of another man, nor ask another man to live for mine."[41] The individual's first (moral) obligation is to promote and enhance his or her own life prospects. Rand is being very serious when she describes selfishness as a virtue. Unfortunately, as Rand sees things, the experience of several centuries of Christianity and collectivist politics has enrolled the vast majority of persons in the cult of self-sacrifice, teaching them to regard true virtue (selfishness) as a vice. Rand's aim is to expose this altruistic "nonsense" for what it is—a slave morality.[42] Like Nietzsche, Rand philosophizes with a hammer. She, too, would be a breaker of idols—Nietzsche as capitalist. For her, the will to power is expressed in the creative acts and competitive spirit of the entrepreneur, who seeks not dominion but self-fulfillment. The heroic entrepreneur (no other adjective will do) is the very embodiment of the rational individual. He is the Atlas who upholds the world, but he acts for himself alone.[43]

Rand and her disciples reduce all human relationships to a kind of psychic variant of the cash nexus. Rand, for example, describes love and friendship as "the spiritual *payment* given in exchange for the personal, selfish pleasure which one man derives from the virtues of another man's character."[44] It follows easily enough that selfless motives are not to be trusted. Either they disguise an evil intent or they amount to a potentially harmful self-delusion. In Rand's novels the villains often spout humanitarian drivel all the while they are scheming to reduce the other characters to slavery. Meanwhile, well-intentioned do-gooders (as in *Atlas Shrugged*) eagerly go about undermining the very foundations of their prosperity by denying the significance of the individual and sacrificing personal fortunes to the collective welfare.

The rational egoist, Rand's hero and moral exemplar, inhabits a world bounded by the cash nexus and its psychic equivalent. Things turn out well enough for the cardboard figures who play out their imaginary lives in the pages of Rand's potboilers, but what of real men and women? What does the rational life hold in store for them? When selfless acts are inherently suspect, what becomes of trust and human intimacy? John Hospers provides a highly revealing answer to these questions while attempting to illustrate the dangers of taxation. He tells us to suppose that we have a wife or husband or financé whom we trust completely— so much so that we give that person access to our checking account and all our worldly goods, for whatever purposes he or she may wish to use them. He then asks, "Would you be quite sure that the person you know and trust most would not think of new things she wanted, for which she could use this open account? Are you quite sure that your bank account would not be overdrawn just when you needed it most for some emergency in your life and work?"[45]* Clearly, there is no room for trust in Hospers' world. How can there be when even in their most intimate relationships people remain strangers to one another? It seems once again that we are back in the state of nature, psychically isolated despite the company of others.

*In the course of relating his illustration, Hospers apparently forgets that the party given access to our worldly goods can be male or female.

Rand's moral precepts become Locke's moral psychology. To live the good life, the rational life, is to recreate the state of nature in a market society devoid of spontaneous loyalties and collective sentiments of mutual (political) affection. This is Rand's idea of capitalism, a pure laissez-faire capitalism unknown to history except as an ideal.[46] This, too, is the key to Machan's defense of capitalism as the one social order that serves the objective good. In their hands, the minarchist apology for capitalism becomes a weapon of cultural warfare. Those defined as anticapitalist bear the moral stigma of being antirational and hence antilife (which is to say immoral).

Rand and company launch this accusation against collectivists generally, but reserve a special animus for persons seen as hostile to industrialism. To Rand and her disciples, technological progress (man's conquest of nature, as they see it) contributes immeasurably to the enhancement of life. Consequently, to question or, worse still, to oppose such progress is to align oneself with the forces of darkness. They have nothing but contempt for the counterculture of the 1960s—in their vocabulary, "hippie" is a term of ultimate scorn—and they are not inclined to be generous in their estimation of such respectable establishment pursuits as environmentalism and the antinuclear movement. Evidently, if we are to take Rand seriously, reason demands the conquest of nature whatever the form that victory may take, and whatever the cost. It is a comment on her notion of the good life that she rises to the defense of air pollution and the electric toothbrush with all the zeal of a knight defending the last vestiges of civilization from attack by the barbarian hordes.[47]

Thus it is that Machan's "objective good" comes to embrace capitalism and its cultural baggage—materialism and the Protestant work ethic. (How convenient that reason should bestow its blessing on these traditional middle-class values!) Given their moralistic perspective, it is perhaps not surprising to find Rand and her disciples describing market outcomes in terms of just deserts. Hospers, for example, is convinced that one's earnings in a free-market economy bear "a close relation" to one's effort and achievement.[48] As for Rand, the virtue of her heroines and heroes always finds its reflection in their wealth and accomplishments.*

Where wealth is a badge of moral worth, poverty too has its moral significance and the rich owe no apology to the poor. Still, the poor will envy the rich (egged on, in Rand's view, by second-rate intellectuals mindful of their own incompetence and resentful of what the heroic entrepreneur-industrialist has accomplished).† There is need, therefore, to reconcile the poor to their condition. "Instead of resenting it when individuals or companies make a million dollars," writes John Hospers,

> we should be happy. That million dollars means that there is a prosperous enterpriser who has created many jobs for people and bought equipment and so on (which in turn requires jobs to produce) to keep the product going. A million dollars made on the free market has filtered down to a very large number of people in the economy—and that a product is available at a competitive price, else the consumers would not have bought it in sufficient quantity to make our company its million.[49]

In short, the rich live well so that the poor may live as comfortably as they in fact do. Or, as Hospers himself puts it, "If no one were permitted to have caviar, finally not many people would have bread."[50] This is the familiar trickle-down theory of wealth with a vengeance. Rand's observations on the economic elite are

---

*Is it possible to imagine John Galt or Dagney Taggart going out of business in an unregulated economy? Readers of *Atlas Shrugged* will recognize the absurdity of such a question.

†The resentment of "second-raters" plays a large role in Rand's novels. It seems to me that both the heroic and the villainous characters of *Atlas Shrugged* are driven by a Nietzschean will to power. For such heroes as John Galt, the will to power manifests itself in the conquest of nature (Galt invents a perpetual motion machine), which leads to the character's self-fulfillment as a rational being. For such villains as Bertram Scudder, the will to power has been corrupted; where Galt seeks to create, Scudder lives to destroy, feeding his ego off the ruin of the civilization he abhors. Rand's novels admit no complexity to the motives of her characters. Heroes and villains are what they seem, archetypes of the Good and the Bad.

even more in the way of a sermon. Of the successful businessman she writes:

> *He* is the great liberator who, in the short span of a century and a half, has released men from bondage to their physical needs, has released them from the terrible drudgery of an eighteen-hour workday of manual labor for their barest subsistence, has released them from famines, from pestilences, from the stagnant hopelessness and terror in which most of mankind had lived in all the pre-capitalist centuries—and in which most of it still lives in noncapitalist countries.[51]

Rand's dogmatic view of the capitalist entrepreneur as a Nietzschean superman may help explain the tremendous popularity of her ideas. If Hayek's depiction of the market as a game is less than compelling, Rand's highly romantic portrayal of economic competition as a heroic contest among superior individuals is all the more gripping by contrast. Unlike such calm enthusiasts as Friedrich Hayek and Robert Nozick, who find a logical relationship between capitalism and freedom, Rand views the struggle between capitalism and its critics in apocalyptic terms. For her, and for many of her disciples, it is nothing less than a final contest between Good and Evil, with the fate of the world hanging in the balance. This vision may be fashioned from a rather sorry philosophy and an extremely naive view of capitalism, but it is the stuff of which political crusades are built.

Minarchy and Contemporary Politics

What of minarchy's political future? Like the anarchocapitalists, minarchists trust in the belief that ideas matter—indeed, that they shape the course of human events. On this belief they build their hopes for rescuing the individual from the state and transforming American society. Still, minarchist ideas do not seem likely to have the effect minarchists intend. Already minarchist rhetoric has been appropriated by conservative politicians who know a good slogan when they hear one. Businessmen and politicians alike are delighted to find a Harvard philosopher on their side and have taken Robert Nozick to their bosoms, without necessarily appreciating the subtlety of his arguments.[52] It strains credulity to imagine the president of the United States or the chief executive officer of IBM endorsing Nozick's "utopian framework" of independent city-states, all of them free to set their own social and economic rules.

It must be said that the ideas of Rand and her disciples lend themselves to ideological exploitation. To reestablish the robber barons as captains of industry is to reassert a romantic myth peculiarly inappropriate to the age of bureaucratized multinational corporations. Yet this myth still may serve the interests of corporate managers, if only as an illusion. And Rand's apocalyptic vision of the struggle between capitalism and its enemies offers conservative strategists ideological reinforcement for the war against international communism. It certainly can't hurt that Rand and the likes of Hospers and Machan are vehemently anticommunist.

The fact is that minarchist ideas, especially their critique of the positive state and their moralistic defense of inequality, come at a time when economic and political considerations have prompted a retreat from the social-welfare policies of the past. In this context the writings of a Nozick or a Hayek lend a certain intellectual respectability to what has become, in any event, politically expedient. And in the more ideologically strident and emotionally comforting writings of a Rand, a Hospers, or a Machan, the beleaguered middle class hears what it wants to hear: that the poor are truly undeserving, that welfare is fraud and theft, that the dog-eat-dog world in which hard-working citizens make their way is not without meaning or justice, that there is indeed virtue in selfishness.

Can the Free Market Deliver the Goods? A Note on Capitalism and Freedom

Whatever the fate of libertarian political theory, libertarianism is likely to help shape the climate of opinion surrounding the debate over economic policy. Now that the free market is once again in vogue, such libertarian think tanks as the Cato Institute can hope to guide policy makers away from interventionist solutions to our economic ills. In fact, libertarian proposals for dealing with public goods (such as education) and "public bads" (or externalities, such as air pollution) do not differ greatly from those of the more familiar Chicago school or the public choice theories of James Buchanan and Gordon Tullock.[53] Like these other devotees of the free market, libertarians rest their case in large part on the technical efficiency of market operations. There is little original in their perspective on the economy; the policy of laissez-faire is an old standby among conservative economists. But the case for the market has new appeal today with the general decline of confidence in Keynesianism.[54]

We can begin to appreciate the strengths and limitations of the libertarian approach to economic problems by considering the example of air pollution. Murray Rothbard is quick to identify government itself as a major (if not *the* major) source of pollution. He also notes that air is unowned and hence a "free good" that no one has a financial incentive to conserve. Finally, he blames government for failing to protect individual rights by allowing industrial polluters to foul the air with impunity (and immunity from prosecution) so long as they meet the government's emission standards. The remedy for air pollution, as he sees it, is

> crystal clear, and it has nothing to do with multibillion-dollar palliative government programs at the expense of the taxpayers which do not even meet the real issue. The remedy is simply for the courts to return to their function of defending person and property rights against invasion, and therefore to enjoin anyone from injecting pollutants into the air.

Rothbard is impatient with arguments that claim some measure of pollution to be the price of progress.

> The argument that such an injunctive prohibition against pollution would add to the costs of industrial production is as repre-

hensible as the pre–Civil War argument that the abolition of
slavery would add to the costs of growing cotton, and that
therefore abolition, however morally correct, was "impractical."[55]

Rothbard has a valid point. By substituting regulation for injunctive relief, the government not only tolerates pollution, it
allows those who benefit from a "dirty" industrial process to
impose the high costs of pollution (for example, lung cancer) on
those persons unfortunate enough to live near the factory. But
will his proposal really solve the problem? Rothbard appears to
assume that the courts will be as accessible to the victims of pollution as to the owner of the factory. Yet it is not unlikely that the
owner's resources will far exceed those of his victims. Given this
disparity, it is not at all clear that persons who suffer the costs of
pollution will be able to bear the price of relief.

Rothbard's proposal ignores a critical variable: power. This is
not surprising. Libertarians are inclined to view "power" and
"market" as antithetical terms.* Market relationships are by
definition voluntary. The state, on the other hand, compels obedience by force or the implicit threat of force. In this view,
power enters the market only when the state commands certain
economic behavior, or else lends its authority to private actors
(as when government creates a monopoly). In Rothbard's discussion, the factory owner has no power over those who live near
the factory. If we define power as comparative advantage under
restricted circumstances, however, we can see that he may. He
can exercise that power by stretching out the litigation until his
opponents' financial resources are exhausted. In what is perhaps a
worst case example, though by no means an unrealistic scenario,
the owner of an industry on which an entire community depends
for its livelihood may threaten to relocate unless local residents

---

*Hence the title of one of Rothbard's books attacking the state and defend-
ing the anarchocapitalist position, *Power and Market* (Kansas City: Sheed, Andrews & McMeel, 1970). Rothbard's message is that the state uses power
(force) to get its way; the market provides an alternative based on voluntary
cooperation (contract).

agree to accept higher levels of pollution. In this instance, the "threat" is merely an announcement by the owner that he will move his property, as is his right, unless the people of the community "freely" assent to his conditions.

Essential to Rothbard's proposal for dealing with pollution is the assumption that a "public bad" can be treated as a private wrong. Although pollution affects a wide area and may cause an entire community to suffer, victims are expected to bring their suits as individuals. There is no reason to believe that all such persons would seek injunctive relief, as Rothbard predicts. Some might be willing to tolerate the pollution if the factory owner would provide compensation. In short, the owner would pay to pollute. This solution, which has been advanced by representatives of the public choice school, again ignores the presence of power in the market. It is unlikely that the "buyers" and "sellers" of pollution will be on an equal footing. Moreover, this approach assumes that a market in pollution is realistic; that is, that every human value (even life itself) has its market price. To paraphrase J. S. Mill's assessment of Jeremy Bentham, libertarians commit the mistake of supposing that the business part of human affairs is the whole of them. One is tempted to go further and agree with Mill's explanation of Bentham's error, that it arose from a want of imagination and small experience of human feelings.[56]

Another disquieting aspect of the libertarians' refusal to acknowledge power in the market is their failure to confront the tension between freedom and autonomy. Freedom from coercion and autonomy, the freedom to define one's own goals and to act independently of others, go hand in hand so long as there are relatively few circumstantial restraints on individual choice and action. A market situation in which all parties enjoyed a rough equality would meet this criterion. A historical counterpart might be the early American frontier, where the ready availability of free land offered the average individual an alternative to wage labor. Wage labor under capitalism is, of course, formally free labor. No one is forced to work at gunpoint. Economic circumstance, however, often has the effect of force; it compels the relatively poor to accept work under conditions dictated by owners and managers. The individual worker retains freedom but loses autonomy.

The loss of autonomy is felt in many ways. Some may seem quite trivial. Employees within a corporate hierarchy, for instance, may be required to observe a dress code that violates their own taste in clothes. In that they must dress a certain way and perhaps act a certain way on the job, they are not allowed to be themselves at work. While such things no doubt contribute to a sense of alienation, they are not likely to be treated with any great seriousness by the employees or others. Certainly a more significant illustration of the individual's loss of autonomy is the inability to shape or alter the decisions of management. The middle-level executive, no less than the assembly-line worker, is a cog in the corporate machine; all of one's efforts are directed toward the company's goals, but its goals are not necessarily one's own. In the worst case, the world one helps create may just be a world one abhors.

This problem is not confined to particular firms; it pervades the entire economy. In the United States today, an engineer whose preference is for mass transit may very well end up designing private automobiles, because most of the jobs for automotive engineers are found in that industry. A libertarian may object that private cars win out over mass transit by fair competition; consumers simply prefer the family car to the bus or the train. Our engineer, then, has no right to complain, for surely his preference is to be weighted no more heavily than anyone else's. This objection overlooks the fact that the decision to manufacture private automobiles is made by a small number of persons who control large corporations and who have a vested interest in fostering a preference for the automobile among consumers. Like the engineer, consumers are born into a world they did not make and presented with choices they did not choose. Our autonomy is limited to the extent that the alternatives among which we may choose are conceived by others.

In the largest sense, the loss of autonomy can mean a loss of control over the quality of our lives. This point is lost on most libertarians, who define quality of life in terms of quality of lifestyle. For them, corporate workers who resent the hierarchy of the workplace can always express their true selves after work. In the consumer culture, self-indulgence substitutes for self-determination.

Of course, not all libertarians go in for self-indulgence. Ayn Rand and her disciples have nothing but scorn for behavior that does not affirm the good. It is not unimportant that all of Rand's heros and heroines are truly autonomous beings. Their greatness lies in their capacity to shape the world in their own image. Like John Galt, the hero of *Atlas Shrugged,* they manifest their freedom by conquering physical nature and overcoming the machinations of their collectivist enemies. Significantly, they are usually the heads of large industries. Yet Rand always describes their accomplishments as personal triumphs, as though their subordinates were merely tools not unlike the machines on which they labor. The "good guys" among Rand's secondary characters are dutiful employees whose highest ambition is to serve the hero and help *him* create the world anew. Evidently not everyone can hope to be John Galt.

The popularity of Rand's vision may help explain the fascination of science fiction for many libertarians. In a world of robots and other devices of high technology, as in the novels of libertarian favorite Robert Heinlein, perhaps everyone can hope to be John Galt.* Technology becomes the great equalizer, shattering the hierarchy of the workplace by automating much of the work force. Or else space becomes the new frontier, replicating the function of the American wilderness in providing the individual with an option to go it alone. In the imaginary worlds of science fiction, the circumstantial constraints of the corporate economy disappear. Unfortunately, as Murray Rothbard observes in his attack on libertarian "space cadets" (the epithet is his), their fictions are really fantasies.[57] The world in which we live is the world in which we must look to find our feeedom.

*Heinlein coined the term TANSTAAFL (*there ain't no such thing as a free lunch*) in *The Moon is a Harsh Mistress* (New York: Putnam's, 1966). The expression is a favorite libertarian buzzword.

7

Confronting the Libertarian Dilemma: Friedrich Hayek's Restatement of Classical Liberalism

The guiding principle that a policy of freedom for the individual is the only truly progressive policy remains as true today as it was in the nineteenth century.

—FRIEDRICH HAYEK, *The Road to Serfdom*

THE discussion of libertarian political theory in the preceding chapters has uncovered a serious problem arising from the attempt to abolish politics along with the state. The market society dreamed of by libertarians has been shown to rely on a faulty psychology that underestimates the range of motives that affect human behavior. Consequently, a libertarian order would be vulnerable to an impassioned politics fueled by emotions so strongly felt as to overwhelm the "rationality" of the marketplace. Significantly, most libertarian thinkers do not address this problem adequately, or at all. Indeed, most do not seem even to recognize that the problem exists. Friedrich Hayek is an exception to this rule. In his political writings, we see an attempt to confront and resolve the libertarian dilemma.*

*Milton Friedman is another and perhaps better-known exception among libertarian thinkers. I have chosen to examine the works of Hayek instead for two reasons. First, Friedman is not so well respected by such main-line libertarians as Rothbard and Machan, who are suspicious of Friedman's eager collaboration with repressive governments abroad (as in Chile). In short, despite

Hayek has been warning Western civilization against the collectivist "road to serfdom" for half a century.[1] His writings seem always at the point of despair, lamenting a nearly universal loss of faith in liberal principles. But he is not completely without hope; like some latter-day Jeremiah, he calls to a people lost in the wilderness of false belief to abandon their folly and return to the path of their fathers.

Friedrich August von Hayek was born into a minor aristocratic Viennese family at the close of the nineteenth century. He was trained in law and political economy at the University of Vienna and for a time afterward was a lecturer there in economics. In 1931 he accepted a professorship at the London School of Economics, where he remained until 1950. During the early part of this period his main work was in economic theory, much of it having to do with the theories of money and the trade cycle, which led him into a brief dispute with Keynes. In 1941 he published a major economic treatise, *The Pure Theory of Capital*. The first statement of his social and political philosophy, *The Road to Serfdom*, appeared in 1944. This work was followed by a collection of essays, *Individualism and Economic Order*, in 1948.

In 1950 Hayek assumed a position in moral philosophy at the

---

his defense of the free market and limited government, Friedman is regarded by many libertarians as a closet statist. Second, it is my own opinion that, of the two, Hayek is the better political theorist. When it comes to social or political ideas, Friedman strikes me as being primarily a popularizer rather than an original thinker. See his *Capitalism and Freedom* (Chicago: University of Chicago Press, 1962) and, more recently, *Free to Choose* (New York: Avon Books, 1979), which was a tie-in to Friedman's series on capitalism aired by public television. While Friedman writes for the general public, Hayek, for reasons I explain below, writes primarily for an intellectual audience. Hayek is less the propagandist and more the serious philosopher, intent on reestablishing the theoretical foundations of classical liberalism. He is not a self-professed libertarian. In fact, he is well respected by intellectuals spread across the right wing of American politics, and libertarians are not alone in claiming him as a mentor. Yet I think it fair to place him in (or at any rate nearest) the libertarian camp. His ambition, as I discuss in this chapter, is to restore the intellectual authority of liberal ideals. Hayek spurns the label "conservative" and claims to have rejected the term "libertarian" primarily on aesthetic grounds. In so far as he accepts an ideological tag, he calls himself an Old Whig. See his essay "Why I Am Not a Conservative," appended to *The Constitution of Liberty*.

University of Chicago. During his tenure there he published a treatise on theoretical psychology, *The Sensory Order* (1952); a book on the methodology of the social sciences, *The Counter-Revolution of Science* (1952); and a major work in political philosophy, *The Constitution of Liberty* (1960). He returned to Europe in 1962 as professor of economics at the University of Freiburg, in West Germany. Since that time he has published two volumes of collected essays on philosophy, politics, economics, and the history of ideas, and a three-volume restatement of liberal social and political theory collectively titled *Law, Legislation, and Liberty* (1973–79). Hayek was awarded a Nobel prize in economics in 1974. He is currently professor emeritus at both the University of Chicago and the University of Freiburg.[2]

Hayek may be described as a social conservative. He is aware that to succeed a liberal market order requires a solid cultural foundation rooted in the beliefs, habits, and customary practices of ordinary people. As a result he shows great regard for tradition and grieves to see it rashly overturned. His is the Burkean conviction that "when antient opinions and rules of life are taken away, the loss cannot possibly be estimated. From that moment we have no compass to govern us; nor can we know distinctly to what port we steer."[3] In Hayek's view, the subversion of traditional beliefs has set modern society adrift dangerously near the shoals of a socialist state, and he labors to bring it back on the course charted by the great liberal theorists of the past.

His political writings are devoted to a restatement of classical liberalism, which he thinks sadly neglected by the present generation of scholars. Although one of his books, *The Road to Serfdom*, enjoyed a wide popular audience (especially in the United States), Hayek generally does not write for the masses. Rather, he addresses his arguments to a broadly defined audience of intellectuals in the belief that mass opinion is received largely from the intelligentsia. As far as Hayek is concerned, it was the defection of the intellectuals to socialism in the twentieth century that undermined the liberal tradition within the general public; he stakes the possibility of a liberal revival on their return to the fold.[4]

But Hayek is no mere historian of ideas. He is a combatant in the war of ideas, waging a campaign for the hearts and minds of his readers. In this regard, it is significant that his style of argument is characteristically defensive. He seeks to inspire renewed admiration for the liberal ideal of a free society, yet his restatement of the liberal concept of freedom quickly becomes an awkward justification of inequality and an ideologically strident defense of the market order against charges that it is oppressive and exploitive.[5] In like manner he extols the rule of law as the concept at the very heart of the liberal polity, but declares it incompatible with political democracy and demands that we choose one or the other.[6] Ultimately, Hayek's vindication of classical liberalism turns into a harsh protest against the democratic state and a repudiation of the quest for a more egalitarian society.

Hayek on Liberty

Hayek begins his major restatement of the liberal tradition, *The Constitution of Liberty,* by explaining what freedom is and what it is not. Liberty or freedom (he uses the terms interchangeably), as known to classical liberalism, is said to be "that condition of men in which coercion of some by others is reduced as much as possible in society." He insists that contrary to popular opinion and the claims of several modern theorists, freedom does *not* mean physical mobility, or having a choice of several alternatives, or possessing the right to vote or to run for elected office, or mastery of one's passions, or having the power to do just as one pleases. According to Hayek, these misconceptions have done much to undermine our commitment to the liberal order. Having mistaken liberty for something else, we tend wrongly to measure our freedom by what we accomplish, and in consequence to regard anything that frustrates our efforts to achieve all that we desire as an infringement of our liberty. Hayek seems most upset by our tendency to associate freedom with the possession of material resources. It is to this belief, which he deems erroneous, that he attributes the political demand for a redistribution of wealth.[7]

Hayek would have us understand freedom not in terms of our capacity to act in the world but as an attribute of the relationship between mutually autonomous actors. All that this conception of freedom requires is that one be allowed to act for a purpose of one's own choosing; whether one achieves one's goal, or even has a selection of realizable goals from which to choose, is irrelevant from the standpoint of liberty. Freedom is abridged when one is forcibly coerced, deceived, or otherwise manipulated in such a way that one's conduct suits not one's own purposes but someone else's.[8] It is an important aspect of Hayek's concept of freedom that a person can experience a loss of liberty only through the *deliberate* intervention of another person. Coercion is by definition an intentional act. Hence it is technically incorrect to speak of an accidental or circumstantial loss of freedom. Hayek explains that we may find ourselves *compelled* by circumstances to do this or that, but this influence on our conduct is morally neutral and of no consequence to our liberty.[9]

What does Hayek mean by circumstance? One example is a sudden storm that interrupts a summer picnic. Mindless nature cannot intend that we abandon the meadow and seek shelter from the rain, though we may feel compelled to do so. The storm has no effect on our freedom, because we have not been made to serve another person's will against our own. But Hayek does not restrict this argument to circumstances imposed by nature. He contends that our position in society may also be the result of circumstances no one intended to create. Even though these circumstances may drastically affect our lives, they do not affect our freedom. Hayek illustrates this point with the following example:

> Even if the threat of starvation to me and perhaps to my family impels me to accept a distasteful job at a very low wage, even if I am "at the mercy" of the only man willing to employ me, I am not coerced by him or anybody else. So long as the act that has placed me in my predicament is not aimed at making me do or not do specific things, so long as the intent of the act that harms me is not to make me serve another person's ends, its effect on my freedom is not different from that of any natural calamity—a

fire or a flood that destroys my house or an accident that harms
my health.[10]

The example may seem intended to prove still another of Hayek's points, that "we may be free and yet miserable."[11] In fact it
is directed against the charge that market relationships are not
perfectly voluntary and that economic power is a threat to liberty. As the example makes clear, Hayek is able to defend market
relationships, even in a worst case situation, by relying on a
definition of coercion that demands evidence of an intention forcibly to manipulate another's actions for one's own purposes.
Like the picnickers caught in the downpour of our earlier example, the unfortunate individual compelled to accept the only job he
can find becomes a victim of circumstance. However, Hayek has
not met the charge that normal operation of the market system-
atically places an entire class of persons (wage earners) in circumstances that compel them to accept the terms and conditions of
labor dictated by those who offer work. While it is true that
individuals are formally free to seek better jobs or to withhold
their labor in the hope of receiving higher wages, in the long run
their position in the market works against them; they cannot live
if they do not find employment. When circumstances regularly
bestow a relative disadvantage on one class of persons in their
dealings with another class, members of the advantaged class
have little need of coercive measures to get what they want.[12]
  While Hayek is not troubled by the exercise of economic
power in the relationship between employers and employees, he
does see the threat of coercion in the case of monopoly, at least
under certain conditions. Apparently he has no quarrel with monopoly per se.

> So long as the services of a particular person are not crucial to
> my existence or the preservation of what I most value, the con-
> ditions he [the monopolist] exacts for rendering these services
> cannot properly be called "coercion." A monopolist could exer-
> cise true coercion . . . if he were, say, the owner of a spring in
> an oasis. Let us say that other persons settled there on the as-
> sumption that water would always be available at a reasonable

price and then found, perhaps because a spring dried up, they
had no choice but to do whatever the owner of the spring de-
manded of them if they were to survive: here would be a clear
case of coercion.[13]

A clear case of coercion, indeed; or is it? On inspection there
seems to be little difference between this example and the earlier
example of the unfortunate employee "at the mercy" of his employer. In both cases people are compelled by circumstances not
of anyone's making to meet the demands imposed by the only
individual willing and able to offer them the means of subsistence. It is difficult to understand why, if the first is not an
example of coercion, the second is.*

In the example of the spring at the oasis, Hayek alters his
definition of coercion. The owner of the spring is said to act
coercively, yet there is no indication that he has forced his customers to serve his purposes and not their own. Why is this an
invasion of their liberty? Hayek's only answer appears to be that
since the water is necessary to their survival, they have no choice
but to meet any demand put to them by the monopolist. To
make this argument consistent with his original definition of
coercion, Hayek would have to assume that under these circumstances the owner of the spring will be unable to resist deliberately manipulating his customers. But Hayek does not say this,
and indeed there seems to be little basis for such a claim. As it
stands, the example of the spring suggests instead that the context of an action may determine whether or not it is coercive.

A further innovation is Hayek's statement that a demand under circumstances threatening to the preservation of what one
most values is just as coercive as a demand made unavoidable by
a threat to one's existence. The problem here is that different

---

*Libertarian scholar Ronald Hamowy faults Hayek for imposing illegitimate
restrictions on freedom of contract in order to make the monopolist appear
coercive. Hamowy argues that in the example of the spring at the oasis, the
only "reasonable" price for the water is that which the buyers and the seller
agree to. See Hamowy, "Freedom and the Rule of Law in F. A. Hayek," *Il
Politico* 36(1972):352–55.

persons will value different things. How are we to weigh claims concerning essential values? Consider the following: If I most value my leisure, but find I must work to obtain the means of subsistence, would I be justified in accusing my employer of coercion? Under Hayek's modified definition of coercion, it appears the answer would have to be yes.[14] Indeed, to pursue this line of argument is to discover coercion anywhere and everywhere one looks for it. Clearly, given his concern with delimiting the concept of liberty, this result cannot be what Hayek intends.

A careful reading of his chapter "Coercion and the State" in *The Constitution of Liberty* suggests that Hayek loosens his definition of coercion not to broaden the concept of freedom but to establish the contextual grounds for legitimate state intervention in private conduct. Following the classical liberal formula, Hayek argues that the state is justified in using coercion to prohibit coercive acts by private parties.[15] In elaborating his notion of coercion, however, he concedes that not all instances of force or fraud are equally coercive. "There are many degrees of coercion," he explains, and not all require government intervention.

> In some degree all close relationships between men, whether they are tied to one another by affection, economic necessity, or physical circumstances (such as on a ship or an expedition), provide opportunities for coercion. The conditions of personal domestic service, like all more intimate relations, undoubtedly offer opportunities for coercion of a particularly oppressive kind and are, in consequence, felt as restrictions on personal liberty. And a morose husband, a nagging wife, or a hysterical mother may make life intolerable unless their every mood is obeyed. But here society can do little to protect the individual beyond making such associations with others truly voluntary. Any attempt to regulate these intimate associations further would clearly involve such far-reaching restrictions on choice and conduct as to produce ever greater coercion: *If people are to be free to choose their associates and intimates, the coercion that arises from voluntary association cannot be the concern of government.*[16]

What, then, is properly the concern of government? For Hayek, government exists to protect *socially defined spheres* of individual liberty. He maintains that, historically, the acceptance of private property was the first step toward the demarcation of these private spheres; from the recognition of property rights flowed a broader conception of individual rights. Today these rights are secure even to those without property.

> In modern society . . . the essential requisite for the protection of the individual against coercion is not that he possess property but that the material means which enable him to pursue any plan of action should not be all in the exclusive control of one agent. It is one of the accomplishments of modern society that freedom may be enjoyed by a person with practically no property of his own (beyond personal belongings like clothing—and even these can be rented) and that we can leave the care of the property that serves our needs largely to others. *The important point is that the property should be sufficiently dispersed so that the individual is not dependent on particular persons who alone can provide him with what he needs or who alone can employ him.*[17]

Hayek's example of the spring at the oasis can now be seen to illustrate the type of situation where government intervention is not only legitimate but necessary. Although a strict contractarian might object that the exchange between the owner of the spring and his thirsty customers is formally voluntary, Hayek does not consider it the kind of "voluntary association" that government ought to let alone. On the contrary, this type of monopoly is incompatible with liberty because it destroys the minimal degree of personal autonomy required to make freedom meaningful.

In refining his notion of coercion Hayek unwittingly reveals an essential flaw in the libertarian conception of liberty. A purely formal definition of the sort Hayek initially proposes, in which freedom is described as the absence of (deliberate) coercion, cannot guarantee any measure of genuine autonomy. As in Hayek's example of the spring at the oasis, a formally free individual may be effectively coerced by the monopolist whether or not the latter intends to take advantage of their relationship. It is the dependence of the customer on the supplier that matters. In effect

Hayek is saying that where circumstance creates dependency—at least in those cases where life or essential values hang in the balance—liberty is compromised. This seems reasonable; but what possible basis does Hayek have for making such a claim? On consideration, it would appear that in refining his notion of coercion he has smuggled in a caveat regarding personal autonomy not found in his original definition of freedom. The theoretical confusion thus introduced is in no way lessened by Hayek's seemingly unjustified distinction between the monpolist who controls the spring at the oasis and the employer of the worst case example who also enjoys a de facto monopoly. Hayek makes autonomy a measure of liberty in the one instance but not in the other. To retain this inconsistency is to impose a double standard in regard to freedom.

Hayek is willing to acknowledge only that freedom is not absolute. As he sees things, the sphere of individual liberty is properly bounded as well as protected by law. Hayek conceives of law as a set of abstract and general rules informing people of what they must not do, or rather of what they must refrain from doing if they are to avoid the coercive powers of the state. Of course, sometimes the state employs coercion to make us perform particular actions. Taxation and compulsory military service are notable examples. Hayek accepts these measures without complaint, explaining that, although here conformity with the law does not allow one to avoid coercion by the state, taxes and compulsory service "are at least predictable and are enforced irrespective of how the individual would otherwise employ his energies; this deprives them largely of the evil nature of coercion." The knowledge that one will have to pay a certain amount in taxes and serve a set length of time in the military still allows the individual to follow a general plan of life of his or her own making. In this way, according to Hayek, the individual remains "as independent of the will of another person as men have learned to be in society."[18]

More dogmatic libertarians find Hayek's position obnoxious and argue that his pragmatic compromise with the state places no limits on what a government may require of its citizens.[19] In fact

Hayek does not impose any a priori limit to state intervention. He assumes that the sphere of individual liberty to be protected by government will in every society be defined by the beliefs and values of the members. Hence a society that does not subscribe to the liberal ideal of toleration may well proscribe certain beliefs thought to be harmful to the community. Hayek insists that "the enforcement of religious conformity, for instance, was a legitimate object of government when people believed in the collective responsibility of the community toward some deity and it was thought that the sins of any member would be visited upon all."[20] This view places him at odds not only with contemporary libertarian doctrine but also with the traditional liberal position mapped out by J. S. Mill in *On Liberty*. Unlike Mill, Hayek is a cultural relativist for whom differing value systems play functionally equivalent roles in their respective societies. All value systems, according to Hayek, provide rules of right conduct essential to maintaining an overall social order and therefore ought not to be tampered with, for the result could be catastrophic.[21]

Ultimately Hayek's commitment to liberal values is contingent on the existence of a liberal social order where such values "make sense." His discussion of liberty may well be understood as an attempt to remind his audience just where they live and what they owe to the free society that they so easily take for granted. Given an audience more attuned to Locke than to Burke, it is not surprising to find that the argument on behalf of freedom running throughout *The Constitution of Liberty* is less traditionalist than utilitarian. Repeatedly Hayek tells us that freedom is desirable because it is useful. It is useful because the free-market economy is an extremely efficient mechanism for generating wealth. In this regard, to which Hayek grants no little importance, our freedom and our material well-being are inextricably linked.[22] Then, too, like Mill before him, Hayek discovers great social utility in the freedom to experiment with different lifestyles, and even different values, on the grounds that we cannot know in advance which innovations may prove generally beneficial to the entire society (i.e., better enable the group to survive or enhance the quality of human existence).[23] Of course, we are not obliged to condone, much less embrace, practices we find repugnant. "But where private practices cannot affect anybody but the voluntary adult actors, the mere dislike of what is being done by others, or even knowledge that others harm themselves by what they do, provides no legitimate ground for coercion."[24]

By resting the case for personal freedom on its contributions to the well-being of the entire society, Hayek attempts to reconcile individual self-interest and the common good. He praises the free market not because it makes possible great fortunes but because it results in a higher standard of living for everyone.[25] Similarly, he endorses toleration because experiments in living carried out by a few rugged individualists may turn out to benefit the whole community. Significantly, this bridge between liberty and community also provides a defense of inequality. The gap between rich and poor is justified by the fact that even the poorest wretches are better off in a free-market system, where they benefit from all the improvements in the quality of life it makes possible, than they would be any place else. That the rich and the poor do not share equally in the enjoyment of these improvements is of no consequence. Hayek portrays the wealthy as the advance guard in an army of consumers. He assures us that today's luxury good is tomorrow's commonplace household item; "the comparatively wealthy are thus merely somewhat ahead of the rest in the material advantages they enjoy." In fact, the rich "perform a necessary service" by experimenting with new styles of living "not yet accessible to the poor" and without which the advance of the poor would be much slower.[26]

Having made this argument, Hayek expresses the well-justified fear that it will appear to some readers "as a piece of far-fetched and cynical apologetics."[27] In fairness, any critic does Hayek a disservice in doubting his sincerity. Within the theoretical framework he devises, capitalism needs no apology. Still, theoretical elegance will not transform economic necessity into freedom or restore lost autonomy. Persons compelled by circumstances have lost control of their lives just as surely as the victims of coercion. What purpose does it accomplish to distinguish between them, except to still complaints against the "impersonal" operation of the market and the persistence of class differences? In the final analysis, Hayek's concept of negative freedom ("freedom from") legitimates degrees of positive freedom ("freedom to") that vary according to the wealth and resources at the disposal of the actors.

Hayek's Burkean Defense of the Liberal Social Order

Hayek's complaint against would-be social and political reformers will sound familiar to readers of Edmund Burke's *Reflections on the Revolution in France*. Hayek shares with Burke a profound distrust of our ability to manipulate the social world rationally. To claim that men and women can deliberately construct a new society seems to him, as it did to Burke, a striking example of human vanity—reason simply isn't up to the task. Like Burke, Hayek understands a mature social order to be the product of generational experience in which the final outcome was never planned and could hardly have been foreseen. In Hayek's view, the extreme complexity of this evolutionary process far exceeds the grasp of any one mind. All the individual can hope to achieve is an appreciation of its complexity. In short, we must learn to accept the functional significance of institutions and behaviors we had no hand in creating and whose purpose we may not fully comprehend. Fortunately for all concerned, the collective experience of many generations has produced guides to right action passed down as custom, habit, and Burkean "prejudice." These rules of conduct, perpetuated because they have proven advantageous in the pursuit of human ends, make good the defect in human reason. In Burke's judgment, which Hayek may be thought to approve, the individual is prone to folly but the species is wise.[28]

Hayek identifies his view of society with what he calls the tradition of "evolutionary rationalism." This tradition is said to include such thinkers as Burke, Bernard Mandeville, David Hume, Adam Smith, and Adam Ferguson.[29] What Hayek claims to have learned from their writings is that social institutions are largely accidental. Men and women do not consciously set out to create the practices and values that define their society; rather, these things grow out of people's experiences in dealing with one another. That is, they evolve *spontaneously*. Hayek is fond of expressing this notion in the words of Adam Ferguson, who described society as "the result of human action, but not of human design."[30] The opposite view, that all social institutions are the deliberate result of human invention, Hayek refers to as the "constructivist" perspective. This view, too, represents an intellectual tradition, the tradition of "constructivist rationalism," which he associates with Cartesian philosophy and French political thought generally.[31] Hayek insists that evolutionary rationalism is sociologically correct, while constructivist rationalism is false; he laments that, nevertheless, over the centuries the latter has been a prolific source of wrongheaded ideas about social reform.

In his early writings Hayek associated constructivist rationalism with what he called the "engineering mentality," the tendency to view social reform as akin to a construction project. What the engineering mentality overlooks is that no social planner has a knowledge of society equivalent to the engineer's knowledge of the limited project at hand. In fact, and this is a consistent objection from Hayek, no human being could ever hope to possess such knowledge; the sheer volume of data required far exceeds the limited capacity of the human mind to process information.[32] Since no one can know all the particular bits of data that constitute the sum total of knowledge available to the society, the planner must work at least partially in the dark. Unknown data represent lost opportunities that cannot be made a part of the plan, and so its efficiency is impaired. Moreover, if the plan is to work at all, individual behavior must be brought into conformity with the planner's vision; there is no room for initiatives that originate outside the approved design. This prohibition effectively stifles innovation. At worst, it allows planning to degenerate into tyranny. The moral failing of the engineering mentality is that it tends to conceive of men and women as mere tools at the disposal of the social planner.[33]

In the first volume of *Law, Legislation, and Liberty* Hayek explains that persons laboring under the false presumptions of constructivist rationalism miss the distinction between what he calls "made orders" and "spontaneous orders."[34] When applied to social institutions, the former term refers to human associations deliberately created for express purposes; the latter describes the order resulting from adherence to general and abstract rules of social conduct that have been tailored by experience and learned through an undirected process of mutual adaptation within the group. Unlike the made order, the spontaneous order does not aim at any particular result. Instead, by marking the field of human action in a reliable way (i.e., by making the actions of others predictable), its rules facilitate the pursuit of various ends by (relatively) autonomous actors.[35] The unique advantage of a spontaneous order is that it "will always constitute an adaptation to the multitude of circumstances which are known to all the members of that society taken together but which are not known as a whole to any one person."[36] The function of these rules (though not their *purpose,* for they were not designed by anyone) is to promote the survival of the group by enabling its members to deal effectively with the natural and social environment.[37]

Constructivist rationalists err in attempting to substitute a made order for the spontaneous order they do not understand and therefore curtly dismiss as irrational. Hayek implies that this would be a grave mistake for any society, whatever its traditional rules of conduct. Even behavioral norms we may find barbaric may be judged only in light of their contribution to the survival of the overall order; their persistence over time is a presumption in favor of their functional utility.[38] The apparent rationality or irrationality of traditional practices is wholly irrelevant.

At any one stage of our evolution, the system of values into which we are born supplies the ends which our reason must serve. This givenness of the value framework implies that, although we must ever strive to improve our institutions, we can never aim to remake them as a whole and that, in our efforts to improve them, we must take for granted much that we do not understand. We must always work inside a framework of both values and institutions which is not of our own making.[39]

Contrary to what the constructivist rationalists believe, we can neither "synthetically construct a new body of moral rules or make our obedience of the known rules dependent on our comprehension of the implications of this obedience in a given instance," for the true significance of the rule we obey may lie beyond our immediate understanding.[40]*

This is a powerfully conservative argument, for it suggests that almost any tampering with culturally received rules of right conduct will have potentially disastrous consequences. Hayek is no Pangloss, but his approach to social theory does seem to imply that whatever is, is for the best (at least for any spontaneously evolved social order). It is not the case, however, that he considers all given social orders equally well suited to the advance of human welfare; we are led to expect that some will be more successful than others and will better enhance the material quality of human life. Hayek in fact argues that a principle of natural selection operates in the social world, favoring more successful rules of conduct (and the orders they define) over less successful ones.[41] Accordingly, we can expect that over time less successful orders will be crowded out by their more successful rivals.

On this assumption, the case for the liberal social order must be made to rest on a claim of superior utility. Hayek finds grounds to advance this claim in the historical achievements of liberal capitalism. In *The Road to Serfdom* he proudly notes that "by the beginning of the twentieth century the workingman in

*Perhaps this makes clear why Hayek would allow religious persecution in a society that honestly believed in collective responsibility toward some deity. Presumably, enforced conformity is functionally significant from the standpoint of group survival and social stability. In this respect his argument is not much different from Burke's defense of the Church of England in *Reflections on the Revolution in France*.

the Western world had reached a degree of material comfort, security, and personal independence which a hundred years before had seemed scarcely possible."[42] Indeed, the dynamic, wealth-producing character of the free market is an observable fact, and Hayek might well have been tempted to build his case on this alone but for the extent of popular dissatisfaction with market outcomes. It seems that today, as far as Hayek is concerned, many if not most people are extremely shortsighted; they routinely fail to appreciate all that they have for want of that which is denied them. In too many eyes the inequality that accompanies freedom appears unjust, and Hayek worries that the people will demand redress in the belief that this injustice can be remedied without impairment of the wondrous productivity of the market economy.

Addressing popular discontent with market outcomes, Hayek declares that the market can be neither just nor unjust, for the simple reason that it is not an intentional actor. Only the unsophisticated mind, he writes, insists on viewing market outcomes

> as if some thinking being deliberately directed them, or as if the particular benefits or harm different persons derive from them were determined by deliberate acts of will, and could be guided by moral rules. . . . It has of course to be admitted that the manner in which the benefits and burdens are apportioned by the market mechanism would in many instances have to be regarded as very unjust *if* it were the result of a deliberate allocation to particular people. But this is not the case. Those shares are the outcome of a process the effect of which on particular people was neither intended nor foreseen by anyone when the institutions first appeared—institutions which were then permitted to continue because it was found that they improve for all or most the prospects of having their needs satisfied. To demand justice from such a process is clearly absurd, and to single out some people in such a society as entitled to a particular share is evidently unjust.[43]

Thus the concept of "social justice" may be ideologically potent, but Hayek deems it intellectually vacuous.[44]

In Hayek's terms, the market is a spontaneous social order having no predetermined end or hierarchy of ends; rather, the rules of the market serve all actors equally well in their pursuit of disparate and unknown ends. He likens the market to a game in which luck and skill both play a part. Fond of neologisms, he calls it the game of catallaxy, from the Greek *katallattein,* "to exchange." The element of chance involved means that even skillful play cannot guarantee success. Hayek tells us that it is not to any particular outcome that we should look to learn the value of this game, but to the sum of outcomes and the range of opportunities it makes possible.[45]

The secret of the market's phenomenal success as an instrument of material progress lies in its highly efficient use of knowledge widely dispersed throughout the society. Hayek explains that in the market order each individual is able to use the information he or she possesses to advance his or her goals; the process of mutual accommodation through the exchange of data (in the form of goods and services) makes it possible for each to benefit from what is known only to others.[46] It is the efficient use of knowledge and not merely the creation of wealth that Hayek stresses, because he sees the former as the true key to material progress. He writes in *The Constitution of Liberty* that "the rise in our standard of life is due at least as much to an increase in knowledge which enables us not merely to consume more of the same things but to use different things, and often things we did not know before. And though the growth of income depends in part on the accumulation of capital, more probably depends on our learning to use our resources more effectively and for new purposes."[47] In its capacity as an information network, the spontaneous market order is argued to be superior to any deliberately constructed economic order.

Unhappily, the efficiency of the market does not alone provide an adequate guarantee of the liberal social order. Hayek notes in volume 1 of *Law, Legislation, and Liberty* that while the normal operation of the market is sufficient to generate a spontaneous order of a certain kind (based on self-interest and the pursuit of wealth through a process of voluntary exchange), it cannot fully determine the character of the resulting order. "For the resulting order to be beneficial," he writes, "people must also observe some conventional rules, that is, rules which do not simply follow from their desires and their insight into cause and effect, but which are normative and tell them what they ought to or ought not to do."[48] These rules do not originate in the logic of the market process, but come into existence through the peculiar history of a particular society; that is, societal norms are historically specific and cannot be known a priori. It is this body of normative rules that must create a presumption in favor of individual liberty if a true libertarian order is to result. And it is because these rules come to us as custom or Burkean "prejudice" that the heirs to the classical liberal legacy ought to revere tradition.

Of course Hayek, like Burke, believes that a society without the means of change is without the means of its conservation. He advises us that we are free to innovate and to examine critically any existing rule so long as we do not abandon the particular framework in which we find ourselves. He calls this "immanent criticism,"

> criticism that moves within a given system of rules and judges particular rules in terms of their consistency or compatibility with all other recognized rules in inducing the formation of a certain kind of order of actions. This is the only basis for a critical examination of moral or legal rules once we recognize the irreducibility of the whole existing system of such rules to known specific effects that it will produce.[49]

In short, we may pass judgment only on the rule (as it stands in relation to other rules) and not on any particular result it happens to bring about. It is to the overall order defined and sustained by the whole system of rules that we owe allegiance. Innovations that tend to subvert that order are to be rejected.

From Hayek's social theory emerges a highly conservative doctrine in which stability is valued for its own sake. Precipitous change is always bad; it risks overturning socially useful—indeed, from the standpoint of the group's survival, invaluable—

practices inherited from past generations. Abstractly considered, a libertarian order is the most efficient form of social organization precisely because it is premised on the spontaneous invention of utility-maximizing behaviors. Such an order, however, cannot be willed into existence; it, too, must emerge from the historical experience of real people. In this respect classical liberalism was never a "revolutionary" doctrine. On the contrary, it is merely a theoretical formulation and refinement of the "rules" that evolved in the marketplace as men and women discovered the social utility of freedom. Hayek's concept of "immanent criticism" amounts to an admonition not to tamper with this historically derived framework, lest the whole edifice come crashing down around us. Minor adjustments intended to preserve the status quo are, on the other hand, not only allowable, but from time to time essential.

For all his concern with stability, Hayek is curiously insensitive to the subversive tendencies inherent in the libertarian order. As Burke observed in discussing the implications of liberal political ideas, the pursuit of self-interest undermines the sense of communal obligation. "The state," he wrote, "ought not to be considered as nothing better than a partnership agreement in a trade of pepper and coffee, callico or tobacco, or some other such low concern, to be taken up for a little temporary interest, and to be dissolved by the fancy of the parties."[50] Burke foresaw that where politics was modeled on the market, traditional relationships would quickly lose their meaning and soon be discarded. What then would hold society together? Surely not the ephemeral bond of mutual convenience represented by contract. In Burke's view, society ought to be considered—in almost mystical terms—an eternal partnership between the living and the dead and those yet to be born. If men and women are to revere tradition, they must be given an object worthy of reverence.

Much the same observation regarding the effects of a libertarian order can be found in the writings of Karl Marx. It was Marx that noted the dissolution of traditional social relations under capitalism and the substitution of the "cash nexus" as a mechanism for achieving some degree of cohesion.[51] Hayek implicitly acknowledges the Burkean and Marxist commentaries, but he is not especially troubled by what they reveal. He sees the cash nexus not as an attenuated social matrix but as the sole means of effectively unifying humankind without insisting on enforced conformity. Because the market is largely indifferent to personal qualities, it is highly tolerant of personal differences. It therefore offers the basis for peaceful coexistence in a pluralistic social universe.

Hayek rejects the notion that a market order reduces all human activity to "mere" economic behavior and the endless pursuit of material advantage.

> The economic efforts of . . . individuals as well as the services which the market order renders to them consist in an allocation of means for the competing ultimate purposes which are always non-economic. The market order reconciles the claims of differ-ent non-economic ends *by the only known process that benefits all—* without, however, assuring that the more important comes be-fore the less important, for the simple reason that there can exist in such a system no single ordering of needs. What it tends to bring about is merely a state of affairs in which no need is served at the cost of withdrawing a greater amount of means from the use of other needs than is necessary to satisfy it. *The market is the only known method by which this can be achieved without an agreement on the relative importance of different ultimate ends.* . . .[52]

Hayek admits that the market order lacks the warmth and personal relationships characteristic of tribal societies. But he reminds us that for all their warmth toward members, tribal societies are usually quite hostile toward strangers and intolerant of nonconformists. The pluralistic Great Society is simply too large and too diverse to allow tribal emotions. Personal alle-giance cannot hold such a society together, for its reach cannot extend to so many persons. Only the impersonal cash nexus offers to connect what is essentially a society of strangers.[53]

But are the impersonal bonds of the market strong enough to sustain Hayek's Great Society? Will the functional utility of the libertarian order inspire the allegiance of those who play the game of catallaxy by the rules, and in good faith, and still lose?

Irving Kristol, one of Hayek's most sympathetic critics, thinks the answer is no. Summarizing the argument found in *The Constitution of Liberty,* he concludes that "men cannot accept the historical accidents of the marketplace—seen merely as accidents—as the basis for an enduring and legitimate entitlement to power, privilege, and property." Kristol, himself a fervent supporter of the market, finds Hayek's rationale for modern capitalism too esoteric. He voices a suspicion that "it cannot be believed except by those whose minds have been shaped by overlong exposure to scholasticism."[54] Hayek counters by stating that the "revolt against the abstractness of the rules we are required to obey in the Great Society" is a sign that "intellectually and morally we have not yet fully matured to the needs of the impersonal comprehensive order of mankind."[55] Kristol, though, has a point. The stability of a social order that requires greater "maturity" than we possess is doubtful, at least during the period of maturation.

Hayek's line of argument, of course, has its rhetorical advantages; it allows him to portray the critics of the market order as immature or anachronistic. The ideals of socialism and social justice, he writes,

> do not offer a new moral but merely appeal to instincts inherited from an earlier type of society. Similarly the people who are described as alienated or estranged from a society based on the market order are not the bearers of a new moral but the non-domesticated or un-civilized who have never learnt the rules of conduct on which the Open Society is based, but want to impose upon it their instinctive, "natural" conceptions derived from tribal society.[56]

Though essentially a generalized ad hominem argument, Hayek's attack contains an element of truth. Dissatisfaction with the impersonal world of the market order does represent a nostalgic yearning for the deeper relationships of past societies. It might be asserted that the market order, however useful for the satisfaction of our material needs, does not meet certain basic emotional needs; on the contrary, if Hayek is correct, it requires that we suppress them (or as Hayek would have it, grow out of them).

Hayek sees the tension between our "natural emotions" and the "discipline of rules" imposed by the Great Society as a main source of the "fragility of liberty." He warns that "all attempts to model the Great Society on the image of the familiar small group, or to turn it into a community by directing the individuals toward common visible purposes, must produce a totalitarian society."[57] In that case, it is not at all clear how the demise of the Great Society can be avoided. Small groups do not disappear in the market order, nor, presumably, do the allegiances appropriate to such groups. What is to keep such loyalties from spilling over into the market, disrupting the "discipline of rules" that keeps the peace? To look to the state for a solution is to invite the appearance of Leviathan. But to rely on informed public opinion, as Hayek does, is surely to grasp a weak reed. As Kristol asks, who besides those whose minds have been shaped by "overlong exposure to liberal scholasticism" would surrender their emotions to the bloodless logic of Hayek's analysis? In the end, Hayek's Burkean defense of the liberal social order founders for want of a Burkean concept of community.

Hayek on Democracy and Limited Government

Hayek's thoughts on freedom and social order are haunted by the specter of the state. He never doubts the need for some degree of legitimate coercion; indeed, he makes it clear that both personal liberty and the well-being of society require a guardian with the authority to use coercive measures to prevent still greater coercion. But what limits should there be to the authority of the state? And how is observance of these limits to be ensured? Hayek addresses these issues in the third volume of *Law, Legislation, and Liberty,* where he considers "the political order of a free people." His discussion consists of three parts: a critique of contemporary democracy, a statement on the appropriate role of government in modern society, and a sketch of a model constitution for the liberal polity.

What's Wrong with Democracy?

Hayek is convinced that contemporary democratic politics are traveling fast down the road to serfdom. The problem, as he sees it, is that the very concept of democracy has been perverted from majority rule *under* law to majority rule *without* law. Modern democracy sanctifies the will of the majority without regard for the liberal principles of justice, exposing individual liberty to arbitrary invasion by the state.

For Hayek, the term "democracy" is used properly in reference to either of two things. First, democracy is "a mere convention making possible a peaceful change of the holders of power." Though a "mere convention," it is an extremely valuable political mechanism. "As the only method of peaceful change of government yet discovered, it is one of those paramount though negative values, comparable to sanitary precautions against the plague, of which we are hardly aware while they are effective, but the absence of which may be deadly." In addition, democracy is a "method or procedure for determining governmental procedure." In both instances Hayek equates democracy with a majoritarian decision process. The former usage refers to electoral majorities, the latter to legislative majorities. Characteristically, Hayek evaluates democracy according to what he perceives as its social utility. The advantage of democratic lawmaking lies in the legitimacy it confers. Moreover, on the assumption of self-interest, law approved by a majority is less likely to infringe on the liberty enjoyed by each individual member of the group. "The principle that coercion should be allowed only for the purpose of ensuring obedience to rules of just conduct approved by most, or at least a majority," Hayek writes, "seems the essential condition for the absence of arbitrary power and therefore of freedom."[58]

It is of critical importance to Hayek that lawmaking be restricted to articulation of the abstract and general rules of just conduct and that it not deal with particular actions.[59] He worries that to elevate a concern for particular results above the need to preserve adherence to universal principles will subvert the overall order. The grave defect in majority rule is that majorities regularly ignore this prohibition. Indeed, the very structure of most legislative assemblies discourages regard for principle. "Since no resolution of a representative body binds it in its future decisions, it is in its several measures not bound by any general rules."[60] In practice, such a legislature has unlimited power to achieve particular results in the name of the majority.

The irony here, Hayek observes, is that in a pluralistic Great Society such as ours, "true general agreement, or even agreement among a majority, will . . . rarely extend beyond some general principles, and can be maintained only on such particular measures as can be known to most of its members."[61] In the absence of a genuine societal consensus, the ends advanced by the legislature in the name of all will, in fact, benefit only a few. Because ours is a pluralist society in which groups and not classes are the most important political actors, the danger we face is not class legislation but logrolling on behalf of special interests. Hayek warns that "an assembly with power to vote on benefits to particular groups must become one in which bargains or deals among the majority rather than substantive agreement on the merits of the different claims will decide."[62] In short, logrolling becomes the primary if not the only means of securing legislative majorities. The same procedure is said to guide the building of electoral majorities, with political parties being no more than shifting coalitions of organized interests.[63] "Democracy," Hayek complains, "is increasingly becoming the name for the very process of vote-buying, for placating and remunerating those special interests which in more naive times were described as the 'sinister interests.'"[64]*

*It should be noted in passing that Hayek evidently considers some interests more sinister than others. In *The Constitution of Liberty* he has a lot to say about the evils of labor unions, for instance, but he finds very little wrong with such professional associations as the American Medical Association. Also, it is not accidental that vol. 2 of *Law, Legislation, and Liberty* is devoted to exposing the folly of redistributive policies rather than attacking government subsidies to business. While Hayek approves of the latter no more than of the former, he is clearly more exercised by the egalitarian thrust from below than by the abuse of corporate power.

Hayek associates the rise of interest-group politics and the corruption of democracy with the decline of the rule of law. When Hayek speaks of law he does not mean just any statute voted out by the legislature. Rather, to him, a law is a principle or rule of just conduct that has universal application and governs an entire class of actions. Law, in this sense of the term, can but does not necessarily originate with the legislature. Hayek claims that historically law was more often "discovered" by judges, who through such "discovery" articulated the traditional behavioral norms of a spontaneous social order. The true function of a legislative body, according to Hayek, is to maintain and, when circumstances warrant, to expand the framework of rules that define and sustain a given social order.[65] In Hayek's view, we have today lost the distinction between lawmaking and governing. The latter task deals not with abstract and general principles but with "the allocation of particular means to particular purposes."[66] (This sounds very much like what is commonly called "administration.") Our most grievous error has been to vest both the lawmaking and the governing powers in a single body. "To leave the law in the hands of elective governors is like leaving the cat in charge of the cream jug—there soon won't be any, at least no law in the sense that it limits the discretionary powers of government."[67] In short, modern democracy, because it is incompatible with the rule of law, emerges from Hayek's analysis as the antithesis of limited government.

What Government Should and Should Not Do

Though a harsh critic of egalitarianism and of government intervention in the market, Hayek is not opposed to the positive state. He assures us that he does not equate the rule of law with laissez-faire. Far from advocating a minimal night-watchman state, he finds it "unquestionable that in an advanced society government ought to use its power of raising funds by taxation to provide a number of services which for various reasons cannot be provided, or cannot be provided adequately, by the market." Such services include, of course, police protection and national defense, but also all sorts of collective goods (for example, trans-portation infrastructure), as well as disaster assistance and even welfare.[68] He objects only to granting the state a monopoly in the provision of these services.

> What is generally described as the public sector ought . . . not to be interpreted as a set of functions or services reserved to the government; it should rather be regarded as a circumscribed amount of material means placed at the disposal of government for rendering of services it has been asked to perform. In this connection government needs no other special power than that of compulsory raising means in accordance with some uniform principle, but in administering these means it ought not to enjoy any special privileges and should be subject to the same general rules of conduct and potential competition as any other organization.[69]

The primary rationale for government coercion is, of course, the prevention of still greater coercion by private parties. But what justifies the provision of collective goods against the wishes of at least some persons? Hayek concedes that it may look as though the individuals are being made to serve purposes for which they do not care, but insists that "a truer way of looking at it is to regard it as a sort of exchange: each agreeing to contribute to a common pool according to the same uniform principles on the understanding that his wishes with regard to the services to be financed from that pool will be satisfied in proportion to his contributions." So long as each individual may expect to receive services worth more to him than what he has been made to contribute, "it will be in his interest to submit to coercion." But there is a problem with this rationale, of which Hayek is aware. It is a property of collective goods that they often cannot be parceled out in discrete units, and so it is not possible to ascertain with any precision who will benefit from them or to what extent. Acknowledging this problem, Hayek remarks that "all we can aim at will be that each should *feel* that in the aggregate all the collective goods which are supplied him are worth at least as much as the contribution he is required to make."[70] Still, *believ-*

ing that one's gain from the common pool proportionately reflects one's contribution is not the same as having it so. Here it seems that Hayek has betrayed his own argument.

If collective goods are difficult to justify, what of welfare? Interestingly, Hayek sees government assistance to the poor, the unemployed, the aged, and the disabled as a virtual necessity mandated by the dissolution of traditional social ties within the market order. In a Great Society

> an increasing number of people are no longer closely associated with particular groups whose help and support they can count upon in the case of misfortune. The problem here is chiefly the fate of those who for various reasons cannot make their living in the market, such as the sick, the old, the physically or mentally defective, the widows and orphans—that is all people suffering from adverse conditions which may affect anyone and against which most individuals cannot make adequate provision but in which a society that has reached a certain level of wealth can afford to provide for all.

Hayek even goes so far as to declare assurance of a certain minimum income for everyone to be not only legitimate but "a necessary part of the Great Society in which the individual no longer has specific claims on the members of the particular group into which he was born."[71]

Ironically, the necessity Hayek speaks of arises from the normal operation of the market: "A system which aims at tempting large numbers to leave the relative security which the membership in the small group has given would probably soon produce great discontent and violent reaction when those who have first enjoyed its benefits find themselves without help when, through no fault of their own, their capacity to earn a living ceases."[72] This seems a rather disingenuous way of admitting the social and economic disutilities of the market. It is a sign of Hayek's own values and not a logical consequence of his philosophy that he prefers welfare to the workhouse.

Clearly Hayek is bothered by the dissolution of traditional communal relations in modern society. He appears ready to acknowledge that the Great Society, as a web of impersonal economic ties, does not satisfy the individual's emotional needs. He draws back, however, from attributing the sense of alienation to the market. "The widely felt inhumanity of the modern society is not so much the result of the impersonal character of the economic process, . . . but of the fact that political centralization has largely deprived him of the chance to have a say in shaping the environment which he knows."[73] Consequently, Hayek believes that by reentrusting the management of most government-supplied services to smaller, local units, we can revive the communal spirit. Still, his own analysis gives us little ground for optimism on this score, for we know the social world to be largely a product of the market. He is certainly right to disparage rule by distant bureaucracies, which encourages neither trust nor a sense of mutual obligation, but he gives us no reason to believe that the social effects of private bureaucracies are any less disruptive.

Focusing on the public sector, Hayek seeks ways of minimizing the obnoxious quality of government coercion. Decentralization is one measure. Reliance on a voucher system, or direct payments to individuals to be used to purchase services available in the market, is another he recommends.[74] He also hopes that government services will be supplemented by private philanthropy, and he calls for an "independent sector" to occupy the zone between the public and private or commercial sectors. Finally, he advocates that the size of the public sector be limited by a previously arrived-at decision regarding the level of taxation, rather than that the cost of desired programs be allowed to determine the necessary tax revenue.[75] This procedure would permit better control over the size of government and the scope of government activities.

Not surprisingly, Hayek opposes the government's postal monopoly and its control of education. In a change of mind since he last addressed the issue in *The Constitution of Liberty*, he also opposes the government's monetary monopoly and comes out for the "denationalization" of money.[76]

And of course he opposes government intervention in the

marketplace, at least in most instances. He does not oppose licensing, so long as it is not used to restrict entry. Nor does he object to the power of eminent domain despite conflict with the principles of a libertarian order, so long as use of the power is strictly limited by general rules of law, full compensation is granted, and the administrative decision to invoke the power is subject to review by independent courts.[77]

One last exception to the rule of nonintervention involves what Hayek deems to be harmful monopolies. We've come across these entities before in our discussion of freedom. In *The Constitution of Liberty* the monopolist was said to enjoy inordinate power over his customers as a result of his total control of some essential or highly valued commodity. Hayek now loosens the definition of harm somewhat. He no longer speaks of control over essential or highly valued goods, but merely of exclusive control over any good. "Though the majority of the people may still be better off for the existence of such a monopolist, anyone may be at his mercy insofar as the nature of the product or service makes aimed discrimination possible and the monopolist chooses to practice it in order to make the buyer behave in some respect in a manner that suits the monopolist."[78] Hayek's solution to the problem of harmful monopoly is to treat the offending demands attached to the transaction as equivalent to a contract in restraint of trade, and as such unenforceable in court.[79]

While Hayek's limited government is something far greater than the minimal state, it is something far less ambitious than a modern democracy. How is government to be kept from going so far but no farther?

A Model Constitution for the Liberal Polity

Hayek would transform democracy as it now exists into "demarchy," his word for a democratic form of government obedient to the rule of law.[80] To illustrate his ideal, he proposes a model constitution that avoids the structural flaws that plague mose real-life parliaments. He is quick to point out that his model is only a heuristic device and is not intended to replace any firmly established constitutional tradition (though he does think it might prove useful in the design of new supranational institutions).[81] In brief, Hayek's model constitution provides for a strict separation of powers among three branches of government. The power to make laws (i.e., the abstract and universally applied rules of just conduct) is vested in a "Legislative Assembly"; the business of governing the nation (i.e., of developing and implementing administrative policies) is given over to a "Governmental Assembly"; and the authority to decide conflicts that may arise between the assemblies is placed with a "Constitutional Court," which is also empowered to review the validity of actions taken by either assembly. The whole idea is to escape the confusion of lawmaking and governing that in Hayek's view has led to an abuse of power in the Western democracies.

The most important element in this scheme (and the most innovative) is the Legislative Assembly, and Hayek goes on at greater length about this branch than about the others. He proposes that it be popularly elected, but is concerned to ensure selection of a competent body of lawmakers. In consequence, believing that legislation is a task for "mature" individuals, he would restrict eligibility for membership to persons aged forty-five or above. To insulate the legislators from political pressures, he would have each member serve a one-time fifteen-year term followed by an "honorific but neutral" position as a lay judge, "so that during their tenure as legislators they would be neither dependent on party support nor concerned about their personal future." Each legislator is to represent an entire age cohort, and citizens get to vote only once in their lives (in the calender year in which they turn forty-five).* "The result," Hayek writes, "would be a legislative assembly of men and women between

---

*The idea of representation by age group greatly excites Hayek. He expects it to dampen class and other social antagonisms by making age the most salient political linkage. In a leap of the imagination, he anticipates the formation of a national club for each cohort (somewhat on the order of contemporary political clubs), in which members will learn parliamentary procedure, debate the issues of the day, and have a chance to display their potential for leadership. He further believes that such clubs could become an important source of much-needed social cohesion. See *Law, Legislation, and Liberty*, 3:117–19.

their 45th and 60th years, one fifteenth of whom would be replaced every year." This system, he believes, would ensure that the whole assembly would mirror that segment of the population "which had already gained experience and had had an opportunity to make their reputation, but who would still be in their best years."[82]

It would be the task of the Legislative Assembly to revise as needed the body of private law (including commercial and criminal law), always taking care to preserve the inherited framework of rules, to which all changes must conform. In addition, the assembly would be charged with deciding the principles of taxation and all regulations dealing with health, safety, and the like, which ought be stated in the form of general rules (and not left, as they are now, to the discretion of bureaucrats). The work of the assembly would be overseen by a senate of former members empowered to remove sitting legislators for misconduct or neglect of duty.[83]

The composition and operations of the Governmental Assembly and the Constitutional Court receive far less of Hayek's attention. The former is described simply as being much like present parliamentary institutions, differing only in that its authority is strictly bound by the general rules of the Legislative Assembly.* He does not impose any special requirements for membership as he did with its legislative counterpart, though he would in the name of propriety deny the franchise to all persons employed by or receiving a pension from the government. He presents the Constitutional Court as an independent check on the two assemblies. Its task is to block unwarranted governmental action. Much like the United States Supreme Court, it is intended to serve as the conscience of the constitution.[84]

What are we to make of Hayek's model constitution? In the

---

*In normal circumstances. In time of emergency, such as war or natural disaster, Hayek would allow the government a measure of what Locke called the prerogative power, the power to do good without a rule. Of course, this power would last only as long as the emergency that called it into being. (See ibid., p. 124.) Hayek's discussion of emergency powers gives evidence of his desire to make the model constitution practical. No doubt he fears being dismissed as "utopian" and seeks to meet this criticism before it arises.

final analysis, it seems less a guarantee of limited government (indeed, it would tolerate quite a broad range of government activities) than an attack on politics. In his own words, Hayek seeks "the dethronement of politics";[85] that is, an end to the scramble for power and preferment which he finds characteristic of modern democracy. His ideal is a government that serves the good of all but caters to the special interests of none. Like James Madison, he confronts the evils of faction by devising an institutional solution. He claims to have improved upon the design of the American Founding Fathers by separating the articulation of principle from the shaping of policy, thus preventing the subversion of the one by the other. He would not have his legislators tempted by the desire to achieve particular results. Also, he would further protect the rule of law by entrusting its care to persons of maturity and good character rather than party hacks and inexperienced youths.

But would his scheme truly avoid the fate of its eighteenth-century counterpart? This outcome hardly seems likely. First of all, age alone cannot guarantee the character of his legislators or their devotion to principle. Moreover, despite Hayek's claim to the contrary, the rule of law is not neutral: enforcement of the rules may be impartial, but the rules themselves lock everyone into an order not all have chosen and many do not want. Failure to agree on first principles would render the Legislative Assembly incoherent. Still another problem is that the jurisdictional boundary between the Legislative and Governmental assemblies is likely to be extremely vague, for in practice it may not always be easy to distinguish the general rules of principle from the less general rules of policy. Hayek leaves it to the Constitutional Court to decide any disputes that may arise in this area; it is not readily apparent, however, how the court will dispel the ambiguity inherent in any such conflict. Judicial error seems likely to occur as often as legislative error and will prove just as damaging to the rule of law.*

*Hayek assumes that the application of general rules can always be distinguished from the administration of policy. But can it? To take a familiar example from the American experience, the Fourteenth Amendment's equal protection clause seems to be a clear instance of a general rule. And yet the

There is an ironic flavor to Hayek's critique of democracy. While he accurately targets a number of problems, Hayek fails to realize that the politics he abhors is in large part a product of the economic order he defends. The same motives that drive people to seek their advantage in the market encourage them to pursue their ends by political means as well. Self-interest, that great engine of material progress, teaches us to respect results, not principles. (If this were not the case, government would be unnecessary.) In fact, the predatory interest groups that haunt the modern polity, seeking to benefit at the expense of the common good, are the natural inhabitants of the Great Society, successors to the traditional social units dissolved by the market. It is the ethic of the cash nexus and not the resurgence of tribal emotions that fuels the battle for control of the state.

---

application of that rule has become mired in bitter political controversy, for many people perceive the remedy of affirmative action necessary to correct violations of the rule as itself a violation of equal protection. Is affirmative action really reverse discrimination? The Supreme Court has wrestled with this issue in several cases. Its decisions have been met with something less than universal acclamation. Clearly the courts are no better equipped than the legislature to maintain Hayek's conception of the rule of law.

8

Libertarianism and the
Liberal Imagination

There has never been a "liberal movement" or a real "liberal
party" in America: we have only had the American Way of Life,
a nationalist articulation of Locke which usually does not know
that Locke himself is involved. . . .
——LOUIS HARTZ, *The Liberal Tradition in America*

THE libertarian revolt against the modern state is first and fore-
most a campaign for the hearts and minds of the American people. Libertarians take seriously the power of ideas, and rightly so,
for libertarianism itself reflects the power of the ideas that have
shaped the American political tradition.

For the most part, Americans have never bothered much about
political ideas. There was never any need. As Louis Hartz observed in his classic study of the liberal tradition in America,
Locke's descendants in the New World encountered his philosophy as a way of life. They felt no need to articulate their liberal
world view, for its assumptions found expression in the structure
and operation of their social and political institutions. Having no
reason to examine, much less question, their fundamental beliefs,
Americans manifest what Hartz describes as "irrational Lockeanism," a practical commitment to liberal ideals that obscures
the prior ideological commitment.[1]

In America, Locke's philosophy defines the universe of discourse. Other political theories may be debated in the university,
but Locke enjoys a virtual monopoly in the real world of public
debate. There is no popular audience for a Marx or a Burke, and
there is little understanding of their "alien" world views. When

it comes to politics, our free market in ideas is woefully under-stocked.

The uncontested triumph of irrational Lockeanism imposes a heavy burden on American politics. It makes political life a matter of habit or reflex rather than thought. A development of this sort has consequences for the intellectual tradition that informs political life. According to John Stuart Mill,

> when the mind is no longer compelled, in the same degree as at first, to exercise its vital powers on the questions which its belief presents to it, there is a progressive tendency to forget all of the belief except the formularies, or to give dull and torpid assent, as if accepting it on trust dispensed with the necessity of realizing it in consciousness, or testing it by personal experience; until it almost ceases to connect itself with the inner life of the human being.

Received as irrational Lockeanism, American liberalism has evolved into what Mill calls "an hereditary creed" that "remains as it were outside the mind, encrusting and petrifying it against all other influences addressed to the higher parts of our nature; manifesting its power by not suffering any fresh and living conviction to get in, but itself doing nothing for the mind or heart, except standing sentinel over them to keep them vacant."[2]

Small wonder, then, that the object of the libertarian revolt is a return to Lockean first principles. The libertarian alternatives to the modern state reflect the poverty of the liberal imagination. Neither minarchy nor anarchocapitalism amounts to more than a Lockean fantasy in which the state of nature comes true and historical politics is banished forever. In the world defined by libertarian theory, every individual is an individualist, every reasonable person is a rational egoist, and everyone honors contracts. All evidence to the contrary is inadmissible. Surely this is not the recovery of first principles, but a sign of intellectual exhaustion. Far from heralding political renewal, libertarianism is liberalism at wits' end.

Libertarian political theory delivers a caricature of the Lockean original that reveals little appreciation of the context in which

Locke wrote. Locke asserted the rights of property in order to discredit aristocratic privilege. He defended liberty of conscience against the enforced conformity of an established church. He advanced the idea of the social contract as a support for representative government, embodied in the Parliament, in its struggle with the crown. If Locke measured the liberty of the individual against the power of the state, it was because in his day there were no equivalent centers of power to threaten freedom.

Locke's world is not ours. America had no feudal past to overcome. Kings and princes never reigned here. From the very beginning of our national existence, the rights of property formed the bedrock of the status quo. Religious toleration has been the rule rather than the exception, and today the practice of toleration, though imperfect, extends far beyond religious beliefs to include secular lifestyles. Government, framed according to Lockean principles, was never much of a burden on individual liberty. And while there has been tremendous real growth in the size of government, the political power of the state over the individual is hardly more threatening than the economic power of large corporations. In regard to American capitalism, the state has shown itself to be less the master than the servant of business.

Yet libertarians assail the modern American state as though it were a feudal tyrant awaiting the Lockean revolution against the ancien régime. They merely substitute the new socialist despotism for the absolute monarch. Ideologically blinkered, they propose a policy of laissez-faire appropriate to an economy of small shops but woefully naive in an age of corporate capitalism. Their attack on political privilege is contradicted by their reduction of human rights to property rights, which transfer all privilege to the propertied. Their defense of freedom is undermined by their insistence on the concept of negative liberty, which all too easily translates in experience as the negation of liberty.

Libertarianism exaggerates the most serious defect in liberal thought: its inadequate concept of politics. Liberalism refuses to admit the existence of a "public" interest apart from the sum of private, individual interests. From this perspective, politics can be no more than the struggle among self-interested parties for control of the state. Indeed, this has been the reality of politics in the United States, and in large measure it accounts for the policy failures of modern government. Unable to satisfy all interests but lacking a principle by which to distinguish among them, policy decisions are unavoidably incoherent. In the majority of cases, private power determines the public purpose. The reflexive Lockean response of the libertarian movement to this abuse of the state is to demand the abolition of politics.

Libertarian antistatism is profoundly antipolitical. Minarchists would reduce the state to its minimal function as the guarantor of social order. No longer a vehicle for collective action, the minarchist state is almost without political identity. It can hardly be called a public institution, resembling instead one of Nozick's private "protective services" with a monopoly within a given territory. Anarchocapitalists go one step further toward the obliteration of politics by proposing that government services actually be turned over to private entrepreneurs. They would literally dissolve the public realm of collective endeavor by converting its symbolic spaces—town halls, city streets, county parks, and the like—into private property.

Libertarianism aims at nothing short of the privatization of social existence. True to its liberal origins, libertarianism rejects the public life of the citizen in favor of the private life cultivated by self-interested bourgeois individualists.[3] It is characteristic of liberalism to define politics in terms of the state, and to conceive of the state solely in terms of the protection it affords private enterprise. But this position overlooks the broader conception of politics that derives from the classical republican tradition and the ancient Greek *polis*. It denies the element of collective purpose essential to their understanding of political life. Libertarianism carries liberal privatism to an extreme by redefining the state (in terms of its functions) as a kind of private enterprise and moving to replace politics by the market.

In the world projected by libertarian theory the individual stands in relation to the whole not as a citizen but as a consumer. The contrast between these two identities is illuminating. The essence of classical citizenship is participation with others in determining the means and ends of collective action.* The consumer, on the other hand, acts independently and chooses for himself alone. The public life of the citizen fosters a sense of community; the private life of the consumer results in, at best, a fleeting coincidence of interests. Citizenship expands the power of the individual to shape the social environment in collaboration with others. It is a deliberate and deliberative activity. The instrument of citizenship is free speech; its medium is public debate; its object is the creation of a collective purpose. In contrast, consumership requires that the individual confront the world as given. The configuration of the market order must be accepted as a fact of social life. Ultimately, consumers are "sovereign" in the market, but only in the sense that entrepreneurs are expected to respond (sooner or later) to shifts in consumer preferences. Discounting the relative autonomy of powerful corporations, which as much shape consumer preferences as they are shaped by them, the net effect of consumership is to subordinate the good of all to the good of each.

One is tempted to say of libertarianism what John Stuart Mill said of Jeremy Bentham's philosophy, that "it can teach the means of organizing and regulating the merely *business* part of social arrangements." Bentham, Mill wrote, "committed the mistake of supposing that the business part of human affairs was the whole of them."[4] The libertarians repeat Bentham's error. Imagining the marketplace to offer the only significant stage for human action, they lose sight of the broad range of human motives that demand a larger setting. The sentiments that bind the individual to the group strike Murray Rothbard as evidence of false consciousness.[5] Friedrich Hayek deems such emotions anachronistic, well suited perhaps to a tribal existence but out of

*In part, of course, my argument with liberalism is an argument over the definition of citizenship. In a liberal polity, where people are taught to prefer private to public pursuits, what Michael Walzer calls "passive citizenship" is the norm. It requires little more than an occasional trip to the polls. Against this norm, I, like Walzer, urge a more active role for the citizen. Citizenship ought not to be a spectator sport. (See Walzer, "The Problem of Citizenship," in *Essays on Disobedience, War, and Citizenship* [Cambridge: Harvard University Press, 1970], pp. 203–25.)

place in modern society.[6] Envy is the only human passion to which libertarians attribute any political significance. It is envy, according to Hayek, that prompts the attack on private property made in the name of "social justice." Envy, Rothbard asserts, lies behind the hue and cry for equality. All of Ayn Rand's villains are "second-raters" who envy the first-rate heroes and heroines they scheme to destroy.

Ironically, envy is not a political emotion. That is, envy is not likely to generate bonds of allegiance that transcend economic self-interest. If anything, it promotes the egoistic war of all against all. Moreover, as Robert Nozick observes, envy is most common in societies where self-esteem depends on how well one compares with others. In short, envy seems the natural consequence of what Rousseau called "egoism" (as distinguished from "self-respect," which does not require comparison with others). But Rousseau's "egoism" is the product of the very bourgeois individualism that Nozick extols. It results from the competitive anxiety that is all but unavoidable in a world where social status and indeed one's own self-image depend on being able to "keep up with the Joneses." What Nozick and other libertarian thinkers fail to appreciate is the extent to which modern capitalism has institutionalized envy. The consumer culture teaches us to "need" what we want, and to want what we don't have. Envy becomes a capitalist virtue, because it stimulates the appetite for consumption and leads consumers to spend more and more in the attempt not to equal but to surpass their neighbors.

Politics, understood in terms of collective purpose, invites us to consider the public good before our private desires. Libertarians cannot contemplate this notion of politics without perceiving the threat of totalitarianism. They fear the destruction of individuality in the name of a higher good. Ultimately, their case against politics rests on the claim that freedom and privacy are inseparable. Whatever its character, whether totalitarian or not, politics is always an invasion of privacy. It burdens private men and women with public obligations.

Are these obligations necessarily a burden on liberty, as libertarians claim? According to philosopher Hannah Arendt, who looks back to the tradition of the classical *polis,* precisely the opposite is true.

> Without a politically guaranteed public realm [Arendt argues], freedom lacks the worldly space to make its appearance. To be sure it may still dwell in men's hearts as desire or hope or yearning; but the human heart, as we all know, is a very dark place, and whatever goes on in its obscurity can hardly be called a demonstrable fact. Freedom as a demonstrable fact and politics coincide and are related to each other like two sides of the same matter.[7]

Stretching her imagination beyond the liberal paradigm, Arendt invites us to look on freedom, understood in terms of the capacity for action, as the equivalent of a public good, something to be enjoyed equally by all citizens regardless of differences in wealth and independent of one's position in the hierarchy of the workplace. Freedom of this sort is the prerequisite to citizenship. It requires that we define a social space in which private interests (and the interest in privacy) are subordinate to the common interest in an equal liberty.

America's irrational Lockeanism has largely excluded Arendt's broader vision of politics from serious consideration. Yet it seems likely that we will never be able to prevent selfish interests from wielding state power in their own behalf until we develop a genuine theory of the public good superior to the claims of all partial interests. By attacking the modern state but ignoring its liberal origins, the libertarians confuse the symptom with the cause. Ultimately the liberal state is betrayed by its own ideals. Lacking a viable concept of politics, liberalism is without the means of its own conservation. Ironically, the libertarian return to first principles only leads us further from the political alternatives needed to rescue the liberal tradition from itself.

Notes

1. The Significance of Libertarianism

1. See Henry S. Kariel, *The Decline of American Pluralism* (Stanford: Stanford University Press, 1961); Theodore J. Lowi, *The End of Liberalism*, 2d ed. (New York: W. W. Norton, 1979); and Grant McConnell, *Private Power and American Democracy* (New York: Vintage Books, 1966).
2. Samuel Huntington, "The Democratic Distemper," in *The American Commonwealth, 1976,* ed. Nathan Glazer and Irving Kristol (New York: Basic Books, 1976), pp. 9–38.
3. Cf. Lowi's discussion of "interest group liberalism" (his term for the new "public philosophy" of American government) in *End of Liberalism,* pp. 50–61.
4. Ibid., p. 51.
5. Friedrich Hayek, "The Intellectuals and Socialism," in *Studies in Philosophy, Politics, and Economics* (Chicago: University of Chicago Press, 1967), p. 194.

2. The Ideological Origins of the Libertarian Revolt

1. Murray Rothbard, *For a New Liberty: The Libertarian Manifesto,* rev. ed. (New York: Collier Books, 1978), p. 23.
2. Bernard Bailyn, *The Ideological Origins of the American Revolution*

(Cambridge: Harvard University Press, 1967); also, J. G. A. Pocock, *The Machiavellian Moment: Florentine Political Thought and the Atlantic Republican Tradition* (Princeton: Princeton University Press, 1975), pt. 3, especially chap. 15.

3. Thomas Paine, *Common Sense* (New York: Doubleday, 1960; first published 1776), p. 13.

4. Henry David Thoreau, *On the Duty of Civil Disobedience* (New York: New American Library, 1960), p. 222.

5. Ibid., p. 229.

6. Lysander Spooner, *No Treason, no. 6: The Constitution of No Authority,* in *The Collected Works of Lysander Spooner,* ed. Charles Shively, 6 vols. (Weston, Mass.: M & S Press, 1971), 1:17.

7. See James J. Martin, *Men against the State: The Expositors of Individualist Anarchism in America, 1827–1908* (De Kalb, Ill.: Adrian Allen, 1953).

8. Albert Jay Nock, *Our Enemy, the State* (New York: Free Life Editions, 1977; first published 1935), p. 88.

9. See George H. Nash, *The Conservative Intellectual Movement in America since 1945* (New York: Basic Books, 1979), pp. 3–35, 313–14.

10. Ayn Rand, *Atlas Shrugged* (New York: Random House, 1957), p. 978.

11. On the virtues of industrial pollution, see Ayn Rand, *The New Left: The Anti-Industrial Revolution* (New York: Random House, 1971), p. 88. For a review of Rand's doctrinal eccentricities, see Jerome Tuccille, *It Usually Begins with Ayn Rand* (New York: Stein & Day, 1971), chaps. 1–2.

12. *Libertarian Forum,* June 1973. The *Forum* was a monthly journal edited by Rothbard, for a time with the assistance of Karl Hess, and published by Joseph Peden. Publication began in 1969 and continued through the mid-1970s.

13. *Libertarian Forum,* August 1977.

14. Murray Rothbard, "Confessions of a Right-Wing Liberal," *Ramparts,* June 15, 1968, pp. 47–52.

15. Jerome Tuccille, *It Usually Begins with Ayn Rand,* p. 106.

16. John Hospers, *Libertarianism: A Philosophy for Tomorrow* (Los Angeles: Nash, 1971).

17. Mark Paul, "Seducing the Left: The Third Party That Wants You," *Mother Jones,* May 1980. See also Peter Collier, "The Next American Revolution: The Libertarian Party Wants to Set You Free," *New West,* August 27, 1979.

18. Paul, "Seducing the Left"; George Friedman and Gary McDowell, "The Libertarian Movement in America," *Journal of Contemporary Studies* 6 (Summer 1983):47–64.

19. See Alan Crawford, *Thunder on the Right* (New York: Pantheon Books, 1980).
20. Cf. Richard A. Viguerie, *The New Right: We're Ready to Lead* (Falls Church, Va.: Viguerie, 1981).
21. Rothbard, "Confessions of a Right-Wing Liberal," p. 52.
22. Frank Meyer, "Libertarianism or Libertinism?" *National Review*, September 9, 1969, p. 910.
23. Ernest van den Haag, "Libertarians and Conservatives," *National Review*, June 8, 1979, p. 727. On the differences among libertarians and conservatives, see also the articles by George W. Carey and Robert Nisbet in *Modern Age* 26 (Winter 1982) and by Nisbet, Walter Berns, and John P. East in *Modern Age* 24 (Winter 1980).
24. Cf. Louis Hartz, *The Liberal Tradition in America* (New York: Harcourt, Brace & World, 1955).
25. Rothbard, *For a New Liberty*, p. 314.

3. Libertarianism and the Crisis of Public Authority

1. Collier, "Next American Revolution," p. 27.
2. Rothbard, *For a New Liberty*, p. 313.
3. Ibid., pp. 314–15. See also Rothbard's essay *Left and Right: The Prospects for Liberty* (San Francisco: Cato Institute, 1979), pp. 6–7.
4. Rothbard, *For a New Liberty*, p. 316.
5. Ibid., p. 319.
6. Huntington, "Democratic Distemper," pp. 36–38.
7. Lowi, *End of Liberalism*, p. 51.
8. Alan Wolfe, *The Limits of Legitimacy: Political Contradictions of Contemporary Capitalism* (New York: Free Press, 1977), p. 252. This passage is italicized in the original.
9. Huntington, "Democratic Distemper"; Robert Nisbet, "Public Opinion versus Popular Opinion," in *American Commonwealth, 1976*, ed. Glazer and Kristol.
10. Robert Nozick, *Anarchy, State, and Utopia* (New York: Basic Books, 1974), pp. 290–92.
11. Rothbard, *For a New Liberty*, p. 49.
12. Ibid., p. 43.
13. Friedrich Hayek, *The Constitution of Liberty* (Chicago: University of Chicago Press, 1960), p. 137
14. Ibid., p. 18.

15. Cf. Christian Bay, "Hayek's Liberalism: The Constitution of Perpetual Privilege," *Political Science Reviewer* 1 (Fall 1973):93–124.

16. The debate over positive and negative liberty has a long and acrimonious history. Perhaps the best statement of the problem, though not necessarily the best solution, can be found in Isaiah Berlin's essay "Two Concepts of Liberty," in *Four Essays on Liberty* (New York: Oxford University Press, 1969), pp. 118–72. For a perspective more sympathetic to the idea of positive liberty, see Christian Bay, *The Structure of Freedom* (Stanford: Stanford University Press, 1958).

17. J. G. A. Pocock, *Politics, Language, and Time: Essays on Political Thought and History* (New York: Atheneum, 1973), chap. 4; also Pocock, *Machiavellian Moment*, chap. 11.

18. E. P. Thompson, *The Making of the English Working Class* (New York: Vintage Books, 1963), pp. 807–32.

19. Title II of the 1964 Civil Rights Act (P. L. 88-352, 78 Stat. 241), which provides for equal treatment for racial minorities in restaurants and hotels, is based on the commerce power. The statute was upheld on that basis by the Supreme Court in Heart of Atlanta Motel v. United States, 379 U.S. 241, 85 S.Ct. 348, 13 L. Ed. 2d 258 (1964).

20. Cf. Karl Marx, *On the Jewish Question:* "Political emancipation is a reduction of man, on the one hand to a member of civil society, an *independent* and *egoistic* individual, and on the other hand, to a *citizen*, to a moral person" (reprinted in *The Marx-Engels Reader*, ed. Robert C. Tucker [New York: W. W. Norton, 1972], p. 44).

21. Peter Clecak, *America's Quest for the Ideal Self: Dissent and Fulfillment in the 60s and 70s* (New York: Oxford University Press, 1983). Clecak describes himself in the Introduction as having passed through libertarianism on the way to his present position.

22. Jeff Riggenbach, "In Praise of Decadence," *Libertarian Review* 8 (February 1979):22–30.

23. Christopher Lasch, *The Culture of Narcissism: American Life in an Age of Diminishing Expectations* (New York: W. W. Norton, 1978), p. 30.

4. The Philosophic Roots of Radical Libertarianism

1. John Locke, *Two Treatises of Government*, ed. Peter Laslett (Cambridge: Cambridge University Press, 1963), *Second Treatise*, sec. 6.

2. Ibid., sec. 13.

3. Ibid., sec. 19.

4. Ibid., sec. 16.

5. Ibid., sec. 123.
6. Ibid., secs. 123–26.
7. Cf. Richard H. Cox, *Locke on War and Peace* (Oxford: Clarendon Press, 1960).
8. *Second Treatise,* sec. 25.
9. Ibid., sec. 27.
10. Ibid., (emphasis added).
11. Ibid., secs. 36, 37.
12. Ibid., sec. 36.
13. Ibid., sec. 48.
14. Ibid., sec. 41.
15. Ibid., sec. 42.
16. Ibid., sec. 40.
17. Ibid., sec. 37.
18. Ibid., sec. 51.
19. Cf. C. B. Macpherson, *The Political Theory of Possessive Individualism: Hobbes to Locke* (Oxford: Oxford University Press, 1962), pp. 197–211.
20. *Second Treatise,* secs. 78–79.
21. Ibid., sec. 63.
22. Ibid., sec. 105.
23. Ibid., sec. 110.
24. Cf. Gordon J. Schochet, "The Family and the Origins of the State in Locke's Political Philosophy," in *John Locke: Problems and Perspectives,* ed. J. W. Yolton (Cambridge: Cambridge University Press, 1969), pp. 95–98.
25. *Second Treatise,* sec. 111.
26. Ibid., sec. 107.
27. Ibid., sec. 105.
28. Ibid., sec. 151.
29. Isaac Kramnick, "On Anarchism and the Real World: William Godwin and Radical England," *American Political Science Review* 66 (March 1972):114–28. A slightly longer version of this essay appears as the Introduction to the Penguin edition of Godwin's *Enquiry Concerning Political Justice* (Baltimore, 1976), hereafter cited as *Political Justice.*
30. On Goodwin's place in the anarchist tradition, see George Woodcock, *Anarchism: A History of Libertarian Ideas and Movements* (New York: New American Library, 1962), chap. 3.
31. Godwin, *Political Justice,* p. 76.
32. Ibid., pp. 732–33.
33. Ibid., pp. 716, 722.

34. Ibid., p. 723.
35. Ibid., p. 722.
36. Ibid., pp. 139, 140.
37. Ibid., p. 462.
38. Ibid., pp. 174–75.
39. Ibid., p. 562.
40. Ibid., p. 554.
41. Ibid., p. 199.
42. Ibid., p. 741.
43. Ibid., p. 753.
44. Martin, *Men against the State.*
45. On Spooner's role as an abolitionist, see Lewis Perry, *Radical Abolitionism, Anarchy, and the Government of God in Antislavery Thought* (Ithaca: Cornell University Press, 1973), especially chap. 7.
46. *Natural Law* (1882), in *Collected Works of Lysander Spooner*, ed. Shively, 1:9 (pagination follows the original).
47. Ibid., p. 8.
48. Ibid., p. 6.
49. Ibid., p. 7.
50. Spooner, *No Treason,* no. 1, pp. 8 (emphasis in original), 11 (emphasis omitted).
51. Spooner, *No Treason,* no. 2 (1867), pp. 15–16.
52. Spooner, *No Treason,* no. 6 (1870), p. 12.
53. Ibid., p. 17.
54. Spooner, *No Treason,* no. 1, p. 8.
55. Spooner, *No Treason,* no. 6, p. 26.
56. Ibid., pp. 12, 14, 37.
57. Spooner, *Poverty: Its Illegal Causes and Legal Cure* (1846), in *Collected Works of Lysander Spooner,* 5:49.
58. Ibid., p. 6.
59. Ibid., pp. 39–41.
60. Ibid., p. 44.
61. Ibid., p. 46.
62. Ibid., p. 50.
63. Ibid., p. 58.

5. *The State of Nature Revisited: Libertarian Anarchocapitalism*

1. Cf. Rothbard, *For a New Liberty,* pp. 51–52.
2. Rothbard, *For a New Liberty,* pp. 23–24.
3. Ibid., pp. 24–26, 45–54.
4. Ibid., p. 46.
5. Ibid., pp. 1–19. See also Rothbard, *Left and Right,* pp. 6–10.

6. Cf. John R. Commons, *Legal Foundations of Capitalism* (Madison: University of Wisconsin Press, 1957). On the American example, see James Willard Hurst, *Law and the Conditions of Freedom in the Nineteenth-Century United States* (Madison: University of Wisconsin Press, 1956), and Morton J. Horowitz, *The Transformation of American Law, 1780–1860* (Cambridge: Harvard University Press, 1977). For a contemporary Marxist perspective on the relationship between the state and the market, see Ralph Miliband, *The State in Capitalist Society* (New York: Basic Books, 1969). Much of what Miliband has to say agrees with the analyses of non-Marxists. Cf. Theodore J. Lowi, *End of Liberalism*, chaps. 1–3, and Charles E. Lindblom, *Politics and Markets* (New York: Basic Books, 1977), especially pt. 5.

7. Rothbard, *For a New Liberty*, pp. 309–10. See also Rothbard, *Power and Market* (Kansas City: Sheed, Andrews & McMeel, 1970), p. 277, n. 76.

8. See Rothbard's attack on Robert Nozick in *Journal of Libertarian Studies* 1 (Winter 1977):45–58.

9. Rothbard, *For a New Liberty*, pp. 31–34.

10. Ibid., p. 196.

11. John Locke, *A Letter Concerning Toleration* (Indianapolis: Bobbs-Merrill, 1955), p. 17.

12. Eldon Eisenach, *Two Worlds of Liberalism: Religion and Politics in Hobbes, Locke, and Mill* (Chicago: University of Chicago Press, 1981), pp. 76–83.

13. Cf. Max Weber's discussion of means and ends in "Politics as a Vocation," in *From Max Weber: Essays in Sociology*, ed. H. H. Gerth and C. Wright Mills (New York: Oxford University Press, 1946), pp. 77–128.

14. Rothbard, *For a New Liberty*, p. 196 (emphasis in original).

15. See *Cutting Back City Hall* (New York: Universe Books, 1980), by the near-anarchist Robert Poole, Jr.

16. See Rothbard, *For a New Liberty*, chaps. 7, 8, 10, 11; David Friedman, *The Machinery of Freedom* (New York: Harper & Row, 1973), chaps. 13–15.

17. Friedman, *Machinery of Freedom*, pp. 98–101.

18. Rothbard, *For a New Liberty*, pp. 202–3.

19. Ibid., p. 206.

20. Ibid., p. 208.

21. Locke's argument was laid out in chap. 4 above.

22. Friedman, *Machinery of Freedom*, p. 156.

23. Rothbard, *For a New Liberty*, pp. 216–17.

24. Ibid., p. 219.

25. Ibid., p. 221.

26. Friedman, *Machinery of Freedom*, p. 155.

27. Rothbard, *For a New Liberty,* pp. 223–27.
28. Ibid., pp. 225–27; Friedman, *Machinery of Freedom,* pp. 157–64.
29. Rothbard, *For a New Liberty,* pp. 234–37.
30. Robert Nozick, *Anarchy, State, and Utopia* (New York: Basic Books, 1968), pp. 16–17.
31. Ibid., pp. 26–27.
32. Ibid., p. 119.
33. Ibid., p. 110.
34. Roy A. Childs, Jr., "The Invisible Hand Strikes Back," *Journal of Libertarian Studies* 1 (Winter 1977):25.
35. Nozick, *Anarchy, State, and Utopia,* p. 83.
36. See Childs, "Invisible Hand Strikes Back," pp. 27–31. See also Murray Rothbard, "Robert Nozick and the Immaculate Conception of the State," *Journal of Libertarian Studies* 1 (Winter 1977):45–57.
37. Nozick, *Anarchy, State, and Utopia,* pt. 3.
38. See van den Haag, "Libertarians and Conservatives," pp. 725–39.
39. Friedman, *Machinery of Freedom,* p. 185.
40. Ibid., pp. 194–97.
41. Rothbard, *For a New Liberty,* pp. 237–41.
42. J. J. Rousseau, "A Dissertation on the Origin and Foundation of the Inequality of Mankind," in *The Social Contract and Discourses,* trans. G. D. H. Cole (New York: E. P. Dutton, 1950), pp. 175–82.

6. Minarchy: The Libertarian Case for the Minimal State

1. Locke, *Second Treatise,* sec. 123.
2. Ibid., sec. 13.
3. Ayn Rand, *The Virtue of Selfishness: A New Concept of Egoism* (New York: New American Library, 1964), pp. 108–9.
4. Hospers, *Libertarianism,* pp. 448–49; Nozick, *Anarchy, State, and Utopia,* pp. 15–17.
5. See Childs, "Invisible Hand Strikes Back," pp. 23–24. See also John T. Sanders, "The Free Market Model versus Government: A Reply to Nozick," *Journal of Libertarian Studies* 1 (Winter 1977):35–44.
6. Macpherson, *Political Theory of Possessive Individualism.*
7. Louis Hartz, *The Liberal Tradition in America* (New York: Harcourt, Brace & World, 1955), pp. 50–64.
8. Locke, *Second Treatise,* secs. 95, 119, 121, 128–31.
9. Ibid., secs. 95–98.
10. Ibid., sec. 119.
11. See Hospers, *Libertarianism,* and Tibor Machan, *Human Rights and Human Liberties* (Chicago: Nelson Hall, 1975). A similar line of rea-

soning can be found in Lansing Pollock, *The Freedom Principle* (Buffalo, N.Y.: Prometheus Books, 1981).

12. Hospers, *Libertarianism*, pp. 428–29.
13. Ibid., pp. 385–91; Machan, *Human Rights and Human Liberties*, pp. 147–48; Pollock, *Freedom Principle*, pp. 73–75.
14. Nozick, *Anarchy, State, and Utopia*. The path from the state of nature to the minimal state is laid out in pt. 1 (chaps. 1–6). The justification of the minimal state is presented in chap. 3.
15. Ibid., p. 109.
16. See the replies to Nozick by Randy E. Barnett, Roy A. Childs, Jr., and Murray Rothbard in *Journal of Libertarian Studies* 1 (Winter 1977).
17. Nozick, *Anarchy, State, and Utopia*, pp. 67, 83.
18. Ibid., p. 114.
19. Bentham emphasized the general anxiety induced by fear of theft in his *Theory of Legislation*. See the discussion of Bentham's argument in Eisenach, *Two Worlds of Liberalism*, pp. 123–24.
20. Nozick, *Anarchy, State, and Utopia*, p. 67.
21. See Rothbard, *For a New Liberty*, pp. 234–37.
22. Hospers, *Libertarianism*, pp. 12–17.
23. Machan, *Human Rights and Human Liberties*, pp. 222–30.
24. Ibid.
25. Locke, *Second Treatise*, sec. 151.
26. Hospers, *Libertarianism*, pp. 61–62; Machan, *Human Rights and Human Liberties*, pp. 121–27.
27. Hospers, *Libertarianism*, p. 63. Cf. Rand, *Virtue of Selfishness*, p. 91.
28. Nozick, *Anarchy, State, and Utopia*, pp. 149–74.
29. Amy Gutmann, *Liberal Equality* (Cambridge: Cambridge University Press, 1980), p. 160.
30. Hospers, *Libertarianism*, p. 90.
31. Nozick, *Anarchy, State, and Utopia*, p. 160.
32. Friedrich Hayek, *Law, Legislation, and Liberty*, 3 vols. (Chicago: University of Chicago Press, 1973–79), 2:115–20, 73–74.
33. Ibid., pp. 124–32. See also Hayek, *Constitution of Liberty*, chap. 3.
34. Machan, *Human Rights and Human Liberties*, p. 136.
35. Ibid., pp. 137–39.
36. Ibid., pp. 81–82. Rand is cited more often than any other thinker whose work comes under consideration. In a footnote, Machan announces that he is "indebted to Ayn Rand in the precise identification of the appropriate virtues" (i.e., the virtues appropriate to the definition of human excellence he employs in discussing the good life) (p. 285, n. 19).
37. Rand, *Virtue of Selfishness*, p. 17 (emphasis in original).
38. See Machan, *Human Rights and Human Liberties*, pp. 118–19.

39. Rand, *Virtue of Selfishness*, p. 23. Cf. Machan, *Human Rights and Human Liberties*, pp. 74–75.

40. Machan, *Human Rights and Human Liberties*, p. 75.

41. Rand, *Atlas Shrugged*, p. 680. Cf. Rand, *Virtue of Selfishness*, p. 27.

42. Rand, *Virtue of Selfishness*, p. 92.

43. Such is the message of *Atlas Shrugged*. Much the same message, though in far fewer words and stripped of dramatic conventions, can be found in *Capitalism: The Unknown Ideal* (New York: New American Library, 1967) and *For the New Intellectual* (New York: New American Library, 1961).

44. Rand, *Virtue of Selfishness*, p. 31 (emphasis in original).

45. Hospers, *Libertarianism*, p. 326.

46. Rand, *Virtue of Selfishness*, p. 33.

47. Ayn Rand, *The New Left: The Anti-Industrial Revolution* (New York: New American Library, 1971), pp. 88, 139.

48. Hospers, *Libertarianism*, p. 90.

49. Ibid., p. 221.

50. Ibid., p. 222.

51. Rand, *For the New Intellectual*, p. 27.

52. See Jonathan Lieberson, "Harvard's Nozick: Philosopher of the New Right," *New York Times Magazine*, December 17, 1978.

53. See Norman Furniss, "The Political Implications of the Public Choice–Property Rights School," *American Political Science Review* 72 (June 1978):399–410.

54. See Lester C. Thurow, *Dangerous Currents*.

55. Rothbard, *For a New Liberty*, p. 259.

56. John Stuart Mill, "Bentham," in *Essays on Politics and Culture*, ed. Gertrude Himmelfarb (New York: Doubleday, 1962), pp. 112–13.

57. See, for example, Rothbard's column in *Libertarian Review*, March 1979.

7. *Confronting the Libertarian Dilemma: Friedrich Hayek's Restatement of Classical Liberalism*

1. Friedrich Hayek, *The Road to Serfdom* (Chicago: University of Chicago Press, 1944).

2. A detailed biographical statement and a complete bibliography of Hayek's writings can be found in *Essays on Hayek*, ed. Fritz Machlup (New York: New York University Press, 1976).

3. Edmund Burke, *Reflections on the Revolution in France* (New York: Anchor Books, 1973), p. 91.

4. See "The Intellectuals and Socialism," *University of Chicago Law*

Review 16 (1949), reprinted in Hayek, *Studies in Philosophy, Politics, and Economics* (Chicago: University of Chicago Press, 1967).

5. See Hayek, *Constitution of Liberty*, pp. 124–29, 133–42.
6. Hayek, *Law, Legislation, and Liberty*, vol. 3: *The Political Order of a Free People* (Chicago: University of Chicago Press, 1979), pp. 18–27.
7. Hayek, *Constitution of Liberty*, pp. 11, 13–17.
8. Ibid., pp. 20–21.
9. Ibid., p. 133.
10. Ibid., p. 137.
11. Ibid., p. 18.
12. Cf. Philip Green, *The Pursuit of Inequality* (New York: Pantheon Books, 1981), pp. 222–27.
13. Hayek, *Constitution of Liberty*, p. 136.
14. Ronald Hamowy, "Freedom and the Rule of Law in F. A. Hayek," *Il Politico* 36 (1972).
15. Hayek establishes this point much earlier in the argument, near the beginning of chap. 1.
16. Hayek, *Constitution of Liberty*, p. 138 (emphasis added).
17. Ibid., pp. 140–41 (emphasis added).
18. Ibid., pp. 142–43.
19. See Hamowy, "Freedom and the Rule of Law" and "Hayek's Concept of Freedom: A Critique," *New Individualist Review* 1 (April 1, 1961).
20. Hayek, *Constitution of Liberty*, p. 145.
21. Ibid., pp. 62–63, 67–68. See also *Law, Legislation, and Liberty*, vol. 1: *Rules and Order* (Chicago: University of Chicago Press, 1973), chap. 2.
22. The basic argument is laid out in chap. 3 of *Constitution of Liberty*. It was previewed earlier in *Road to Serfdom*, chap. 1, and can be found elsewhere in Hayek's numerous books and essays.
23. Hayek, *Constitution of Liberty*, pp. 29–38.
24. Ibid., p. 145.
25. Ibid., pp. 43–44. See also Hayek's disputation of the Marxist concept of immiseration in his introductory essay to *Capitalism and the Historians* (Chicago: University of Chicago Press, 1954).
26. Hayek, *Constitution of Liberty*, pp. 44–45.
27. Ibid., p. 45.
28. Hayek develops this argument most fully in vol. 1 of *Law, Legislation, and Liberty*, chap. 2.
29. Ibid., p. 22.
30. Ibid., p. 20.
31. Ibid., pp. 9–11; Hayek, *Constitution of Liberty*, pp. 54–56.
32. Hayek, *Road to Serfdom*, chap. 4; *Individualism and the Economic Order* (Chicago: University of Chicago Press, 1948), chap. 4; *The Counter-*

Revolution of Science: Studies on the Abuse of Reason (Glencoe, Ill.: Free Press of Glencoe, 1955), chap. 10.
33. Hayek, *Road to Serfdom*, chap. 7.
34. Ibid., chap. 2.
35. Hayek, *Law, Legislation, and Liberty*, 1:36–39.
36. Ibid., p. 44.
37. Ibid., p. 18.
38. Ibid.
39. Hayek, *Constitution of Liberty*, p. 63. Cf. *Law, Legislation, and Liberty*, 2:27.
40. Hayek, *Constitution of Liberty*, p. 63.
41. Hayek, *Law, Legislation, and Liberty*, 1:17–19.
42. Ibid., p. 17.
43. Hayek, *Law, Legislation, and Liberty*, 2:62, 64–65.
44. Ibid., p. 67.
45. Ibid., pp. 114–28.
46. Ibid., pp. 8–9.
47. Hayek, *Constitution of Liberty*, p. 43.
48. Hayek, *Law, Legislation, and Liberty*, 1:45.
49. Ibid., p. 24.
50. Burke, *Reflections on the Revolution in France*, p. 110.
51. Karl Marx, *The Communist Manifesto* (New York: International Publishers, 1973), p. 11.
52. Hayek, *Law, Legislation, and Liberty*, 2:113 (emphasis added).
53. Ibid., pp. 112–13, 143–47.
54. Irving Kristol, "'When Virtue Loses All Her Loveliness': Some Reflections on Capitalism and the 'Free Society,'" in *Two Cheers for Capitalism* (New York: Basic Books, 1978), p. 247.
55. Hayek, *Law, Legislation, and Liberty*, 2:149.
56. Ibid., p. 147.
57. Ibid.
58. Ibid., 3:5.
59. Hayek elaborates the distinction between the abstract rules of just conduct which define a spontaneous order and the rules governing particular actions within a given organization in vol. 1 of *Law, Legislation, and Liberty*, chap. 5.
60. Ibid., 3:8.
61. Ibid., p. 17.
62. Ibid., p. 10.
63. Ibid., p. 13.
64. Ibid., p. 32.
65. Ibid., 1:chap. 4.
66. Ibid., 3:23.
67. Ibid., p. 31.

68. Ibid., pp. 41–55.
69. Ibid., p. 47.
70. Ibid., p. 45 (emphasis added).
71. Ibid., pp. 54–55.
72. Ibid., p. 55.
73. Ibid., p. 146.
74. Ibid., p. 46.
75. Ibid., pp. 49–54.
76. Ibid., pp. 57–62. Cf. *Constitution of Liberty*, chap. 21.
77. Hayek, *Law, Legislation, and Liberty*, 3:62–63.
78. Ibid., p. 84.
79. Ibid., p. 87.
80. Ibid., p. 39.
81. Ibid., pp. 107–8. Hayek has always found fascinating the idea of a world order built around adherence to universal principles of just conduct. See, for example, chap. 15 of *Road to Serfdom*, "The Prospects of International Order."
82. Hayek, *Law, Legislation, and Liberty*, 3:113.
83. Ibid., pp. 114–16.
84. Ibid., pp. 119–22.
85. This is the subtitle of the chapter that follows his sketch of the model constitution.

8. Libertarianism and the Liberal Imagination

1. Hartz, *Liberal Tradition in America*.
2. John Stuart Mill, *On Liberty* (New York: Meredith, 1947), p. 40.
3. This aspect of liberalism is explored by Sheldon Wolin in *Politics and Vision: Continuity and Innovation in Western Political Thought* (Boston: Little, Brown, 1960), chap. 9.
4. John Stuart Mill, "Bentham," in *Essays on Politics and Culture*, ed. Himmelfarb, pp. 112–13.
5. Rothbard, *For a New Liberty*, pp. 57–58.
6. Hayek, *Law, Legislation, and Liberty*, 2:147–50.
7. Hannah Arendt, *Between Past and Future* (New York: Viking Press, 1954), pp. 148–49.

Index

Library of Congress Cataloging in Publication Data
Newman, Stephen L.
    Liberalism at wits' end.

    Includes index.
        1. Libertarianism.   2. Libertarianism—United States
    I. Title.
    JC571.N48   1984   320.5′12   84–7108
    ISBN 0–8014–1747–3   (alk. paper).